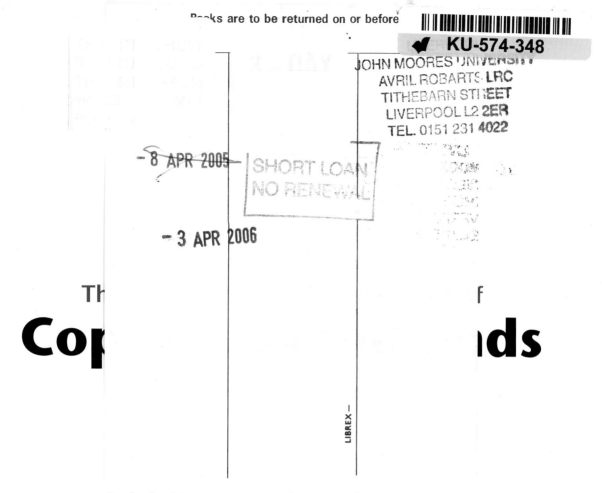

Th... of

Cop...ds

Ralph Harmer and Jonathan Howe

Edinburgh: Forestry Commission

Applications for reproduction of any part of this publication should be addressed to:
HMSO, Licensing Division, St Clements House, 2–16 Colegate, Norwich NR3 1BQ.

First published in 2003 by the Forestry Commission
231 Corstorphine Road, Edinburgh EH12 7AT.

ISBN 0 85538 591 X

HARMER, RALPH AND HOWE, JONATHAN (2003).
The silviculture and management of coppice woodlands.
Forestry Commission, Edinburgh. i–iv + 1–90 pp.

Keywords: coppice, protection from mammals, restoration, silviculture, woodland management.

Printed in the United Kingdom
on Robert Horne Hello Matt

FCBK001/PPD(ECD)/BTH-3000/MAR03

Acknowledgements

The authors would like to thank all foresters, woodland managers and owners for identifying and providing access to sites studied in the survey; Malcolm Robertson and Ian Tubby for assisting with field work; and Roger Boswell for analysing data.

Contents

Overall summary and aims   vii

1. **Coppice in Britain**   1
   Cultural importance of coppice   1
   Biological importance of coppice   2
   Area of coppice in Britain   3
   Tree species of coppice woodlands   5
   Scope and aims   8
   Summary   9
   Further reading and references   10

2. **Coppice silviculture**   13
   Simple coppice   14
   Coppice with standards   15
   Coppice selection system   15
   Current management   16
   Summary   17
   Further reading and references   17

3. **Biology of coppice stools**   19
   The origins of coppice shoots   19
   Biological factors influencing the success of coppice   21
   Silvicultural factors influencing the success of coppicing   23
   Coppice species in Britain   27
   Longevity of stools   29
   Summary   30
   Further reading and references   30

4. **Practical aspects of management**   33
   Management of stools   35
   Restocking and restoration of coppice   38
   Methods of restocking   40
   Harvesting damage   45
   Yield from coppice woods   47
   Uses and markets for coppice   50
   Summary   54
   Further reading and references   55

5. Management of standards   59
Systematic management of standards   59
Influence of standards on growth of the underwood   60
Summary   64
Further reading and references   64

6. Protection from browsing mammals   67
Population control   68
Use of harvesting residues   69
Fences   71
Choosing appropriate protection   73
Summary   73
Further reading and references   74

7. Establishment of new coppice woodlands   77
Characteristics of British tree species that can be grown as coppice stools   78
Method of establishment   81
Distribution of trees   82
Size of new woodlands   82
Initiation of new stools and the coppice cycle   83
Further reading and references   85

Appendix   87

Overall summary and aims

The aim of this book is to give information and advice on the management of trees, stools and woodlands as coppice. This is necessary if coppice woodlands are to continue to produce marketable crops and provide the variety of conservation, amenity and landscape objectives in which managers are interested. Coppice woodlands form an important part of Great Britain's cultural heritage and are often valuable areas for conservation of biodiversity, especially those semi-natural woodlands that have a long history of management. Two forms of coppice were common, simple coppice and coppice with standards, but during the 20th century there was a significant reduction in the area of these coppice woodlands and markets for traditional products declined or disappeared altogether. Many coppice woodlands are now neglected and are classified as high forest, but not all are suitable for the reintroduction of coppice management.

Many native broadleaved trees can be grown as coppice but successful regrowth after felling depends on a variety of factors including size, age and position of the cut. Overstorey trees in coppice with standard woodlands have an adverse effect on coppice growth and canopy cover should not exceed 20–30% at the time of felling the underwood. Prolonged, severe browsing by mammals can ruin crops, kill stools and seriously degrade woodland. Adequate protection to prevent excessive browsing damage is essential. Procedures for restocking within existing coppice and species choice and methods for establishing new woodlands are described.

Charcoal burning in the Forest of Dean, 1909. When complete this stack would have been about 4 m in diameter and 1.6 m high at the centre, taking 8 men 2 hours to build.

1. Coppice in Britain

Coppice is an ancient form of sustainable woodland management which provides both fuel and raw materials. Changes in agriculture, industry and society during the past 200 years have led to a decline in the demand for traditional products that are now either unnecessary, required in much smaller amounts or have been displaced by alternatives. As a result the area of woodland actively managed as coppice has declined significantly during the past 100 years. However, coppice is still an important part of the British countryside and remains of great interest to many people and organisations.

Cultural importance of coppice

Coppice woodlands form part of our cultural heritage and provide a living link with the past, and there is reason to suspect that some are remnants of the wildwood that developed after the last period of glaciation. Maps and other records show that individual woodlands can have long histories retaining similar shapes and positions for many centuries. The types of product from such woodlands are well known and, using relatively simple tools, today's craftsmen can work in the same woodland and produce similar products to those of our ancestors. These products were not only for domestic and agricultural use, they also had commercial roles and were important in our industrial heritage. For example, oak coppice was used to produce bark for the tanning industry, and charcoal was made for smelting.

1

Late 20th century steel kilns producing charcoal from mixed broadleaved coppice woodland.

Biological importance of coppice

Although coppice woodlands may be valuable historical and cultural entities, they are often also important areas for conservation and considerable effort is expended in retaining and restoring their biological interest. A large proportion of the ancient semi-natural woodland that remains today was originally managed as some form of coppice: this has implications for the diversity of the animal and plant communities that are likely to be present and the type of management that is needed. However,

A recently felled area of oak coppice in the Wyre Forest cut to promote the ground flora and butterflies such as the pearl-bordered fritillary. A small number of standards derived from stored coppice or maidens have been retained. The site was fenced to prevent browsing by deer.

evidence of previous management by coppice does not necessarily mean that the woodland is ancient as many coppice woodlands have been improved or established by planting: this was mainly with sweet chestnut and hazel in the south, and oak in the north and west. Nevertheless in most parts of the country evidence of coppice structure can be used in combination with other features, such as plant communities and the presence of boundary ditches and banks, to indicate that a woodland could be ancient.

Woodland management by coppicing plays an important role in maintaining biodiversity. It provides a wide range of habitats across a range of factors such as structure, light environment and age of trees. Relative to high forest, traditionally managed coppice woodlands have a large amount of open space and edge habitats, and a range of tree size and age classes varying from newly regenerating shoots to mature standards. Consequently, the apparent biological interest in a small area of coppice may be greater than for a similar area of high forest.

Although coppice woodlands are traditional and provide a sustainable resource, they are managed and have characteristics that differ significantly from natural woodlands. These include the size and rate of gap formation; the age structure of trees and compartments; species mixture; amount of deadwood; size; and the flora and fauna present.

Many former coppice woodlands have been transformed to high forest and although this trend is likely to continue there are good reasons, both cultural and biological, for the retention of some under traditional systems of management. However, such woodlands must be managed using best available practice otherwise their value may diminish.

Area of coppice in Britain

Data from 7 surveys showed that the area of coppice declined by about 90% during the 20th century from 230 000 ha in 1905 to 23 000 ha in 1997, the reduction being greater for coppice with standards than simple coppice (Table 1.1). While some of these reductions will have been absolute and caused by changes in land-use, such as conversion to agriculture and urbanisation, other management changes that are less dramatic can have an important influence on the area categorised as coppice. Failure to cut trees on a regular basis has allowed stems to grow and whether by design or neglect, coppice woodlands have often developed into high forest. In contrast the loss or degeneration of stools and standards may have caused

Table 1.1 Estimated areas (000s ha) of simple coppice and coppice with standards recorded in surveys made during the 20th century

Year	England		Wales		Scotland		Britain		Total	Comments
	C	S	C	S	C	S	C	S		
1905[a]	215		6		9				230	Data from Board of Agriculture returns.
1913[a]	208		8		11				227	
1924[b]	31	163	7	8	2	2	40	173	213	Based on questionnaires, minimum area of each woodland = 0.8 ha.
1947	41	91	7	1	<1	<1	48	92	140	Very detailed field survey, minimum area of each woodland = 2 ha, needed minimum of 15 standards ha⁻¹ to classify as **S**.
1965	18	10	<1	*	*	*	18	10	29	Field survey, minimum woodland area 0.4 ha, minimum of 15 standards ha⁻¹ for **S**, maximum coppice stem diameter 19.4 cm at breast height (≡ 6"quarter girth). Areas of different types of coppice do not include Forestry Commission's 840 ha, but this is included in the total.
1980	26	11	2	<1	<1	<1	28	12	40	Field survey, minimum area of each woodland = 0.25 ha, minimum of 25 standards ha⁻¹ for **S**, maximum coppice stem diameter 15 cm dbh.
1997[c]	11	10	<1	*	<1	<1	12	11	23	As 1980 except minimum woodland area = 2 ha.

C = Simple coppice.
S = Coppice with standards (for definitions see Chapter 2).
* None recorded in this survey.
[a] In 1905 and 1913 coppice types were not separated.
[b] Figures estimated from county data.
 (Prior to 1924 data for Monmouth was included in totals for England).
[c] Data from National Inventory of Woodland and Trees carried out between 1995 and 2000.

Note: Direct comparisons between the surveys cannot be made for a variety of reasons including differences in methodology, changes in definitions of woodland categories assessed, and sizes of woodland surveyed. The numbers presented should be regarded as indicative of the changes in area of coppice that have taken place. The figures are for areas categorised as simple coppice, or coppice with standards, using definitions which changed slightly between surveys. They can be broadly summarised as woodlands comprising coppice stools with 2 or more stems, that were obviously worked or were on a known rotation, and of sufficient quality to produce a marketable crop or be retained for conversion to high forest. The changes in criteria for number of standards per hectare (ha⁻¹) and maximum dbh between 1947 and 1982 would have tended to reduce the area classified as coppice woodland.

the reclassification of coppice woodland to scrub. Such changes to high forest or scrub will have altered the area of coppice recorded, but for individual woodlands they could be reversed by suitable treatment if managers decide that coppice woodland is a desirable option.

The data in Table 1.1 show that during the 20th century the greatest area of coppice woodland was in England. Most of this was in the southern counties. The surveys took place after the decline of coppice woodlands had begun and the small areas recorded for Scotland and Wales may give a misleading impression of the importance of coppice during earlier times. In the 18th and early 19th centuries a flourishing tan bark industry developed in Scotland. It was based on oak managed predominantly as simple coppice, which was formed by conversion of natural woodlands or plantations, but by the middle of the 19th century this type of silviculture was largely abandoned. In Wales there is a long history of management by coppice with produce from woodlands supporting a variety of industries.

Tree species of coppice woodlands

The species found within coppice woodlands depend on a variety of factors including soil type, location and previous history of management. Of the major coppice species hazel is characteristic of the chalk downland of southern England but it is a widespread component of mixed coppice throughout the country; ash is also widespread, occurring on calcareous and clay soils that are not too acidic; on the heavier, more acidic soils of the southeast, hornbeam is important, whereas sweet chestnut grows on those that are more freely drained; oak coppice occurs on moderately acid soils in many parts of the country. A variety of other species can occur in mixtures throughout Britain.

Management of woodlands as coppice has probably preserved a variety of different woodland types and maintained populations of trees and shrubs. However, the trees currently growing in coppice woodlands have been subjected to a variety of selection pressures which may be natural or aided by silvicultural treatment, for example: the ability of different species to regrow after felling (e.g. birch does badly relative to oak); the longevity of stools (e.g. beech is short-lived relative to hazel); cleaning of undesirable species (e.g. birch from oak coppice); and improvement by planting of desirable species (e.g. oak, sweet chestnut and hazel). Consequently the precise mixture and abundance of species may not always represent that which would naturally occur on the site. The mixture will tend to comprise species which can survive repeated cutting and are light demanding, growing quickly in open conditions.

The viability of coppice as a system of woodland management will ultimately depend on the species present and their ability to regrow after cutting. As species vary in their ability to survive it is unrealistic to expect that all types of woodland should have the potential to be managed as coppice. The regrowth of beech and birch after cutting is often poor and stump mortality can be high, and where these species form a large component of the woodland, management as coppice is probably an unrealistic option. The types of woodland in which management by coppice is most appropriate are shown in Table 1.2.

Many semi-natural woodlands are likely to be managed for their conservation and biodiversity value, but not all stands are suitable for management as coppice and each should be assessed individually using the broad characteristics listed in Table 1.3 as a guide. The decision to use a coppice system should only be made if it meets the management objectives for the woodland. Any assessment of this method should include an analysis of the likelihood of successful regrowth from stumps after cutting and what precautions may be needed to ensure the establishment of new stems.

Neglected stools of coppiced beech which may show high mortality if recut.

Coppice shoots of birch growing from a young stool.

Stools of birch that are unlikely to grow well if recoppiced.

Table 1.2 Woodland types with most potential for future management as coppice

Semi-natural woodland type[a]	NVC	Woodland community
Lowland acid beech and oak woods	W16	*Quercus* spp. – *Betula* spp. – *Deschampsia flexuosa*
Lowland mixed broadleaved woods	W8	*Fraxinus excelsior – Acer campestre – Mercurialis perennis*
	W10	*Quercus robur – Pteridium aquilinum – Rubus fruticosus*
Upland mixed ash woods	W8	*Fraxinus excelsior – Acer campestre – Mercurialis perennis*
	W9	*Fraxinus excelsior – Sorbus aucuparia – Mercurialis perennis*
Upland oak woods	W11	*Quercus petraea – Betula pubescens – Oxalis acetosella*
	W17	*Quercus petraea – Betula pubescens – Dicranum majus* (where these are dominated by oak)
Wet woodlands	W6	*Alnus glutinosa – Urtica dioica*
	W7	*Alnus glutinosa – Fraxinus excelsior – Lysimachia nemorum*

[a]Woodland types listed in Forestry Commission Practice Guides 1–8: *The management of semi-natural woodlands* (1994); not all NVC communities occurring within these types are suitable. See Rodwell (1991) for definitions of NVC woodland communities.

Table 1.3 Desirable characteristics of individual stands of semi-natural broadleaved woodland with the potential to be managed as coppice

Location	Poorly wooded area. Intensively farmed district.
Stand	Small wood (<10 ha). Diverse mixture of woody species. High proportion of short-lived, light demanding trees (e.g. alder, aspen, birch, willow). Animals and plant species typical of coppice woodlands present.
Management	Coppice still being cut. Underwood cut within last 50 years. Damage from browsing and grazing animals can be adequately controlled. Markets exist for produce.

For further information see Forestry Commission Practice Guides 1–8: *The management of semi-natural woodlands* (1994) and Peterken (1996).

Scope and aims

During the past 30 years the importance of semi-natural coppice woodlands as a biological resource has become well recognised, and whilst some recent management may have taken place simply to maintain a historic woodland using traditional silvicultural practices, the major reason for the re-introduction of active management to many coppice woodlands has been to maintain and improve their value for wildlife and conservation. The biodiversity value of such woodlands is often high relative to newly established plantations for reasons which include: long-term, continuous woodland habitat; the mixture of species present, which is generally native in origin; the structural diversity created by regular management; open space – both temporary and permanent; and mature habitats provided by standards and old coppice stools. Detailed discussion of the principles relating to management of coppice woodlands for the maintenance of their biodiversity are beyond the scope of this book, but some introductory information on this subject is contained within the references at the end of this chapter. However, in the long-term, the achievement of conservation, biodiversity and other similar aims requires the successful implementation of appropriate silvicultural techniques to maintain the coppice woodland.

Due to the potential for biofuel to contribute to power generation there is currently considerable interest in the establishment of new areas of short rotation coppice of willow and poplar on ex-agricultural land. The establishment, management and ob-jectives of these new, short rotation coppice areas are very different from those woods comprising traditional coppice species and such areas are not covered in this book.

In recent years there has been a revival of interest in the utilisation of coppice woodlands and products, and at present there is a desire to bring long-neglected woodlands back into management for reasons which include an improvement in the quality of the standing crop, an increase in the value of the woodland to the owner and, as a consequence, an enhancement in the long-term prospects for survival of the woodland. However, the skills and experience necessary to manage coppice successfully have been in decline for many years, but this may not be surprising as foresters are usually trained to manage high forests which often comprise coniferous species.

The primary aim of this book is to give information and advice on the management of trees, stools and woodlands as coppice, which is necessary if coppice woodlands are to continue to produce wood, timber and other products, or provide the variety of other objectives such as conservation, biodiversity, amenity and landscape in which managers may be interested.

Summary

- Coppice woodlands form an important part of our cultural heritage and are often important areas for the maintenance of biodiversity, especially those semi-natural woodlands that have a long history of management.

- The markets for many traditional coppice products have markedly declined or disappeared altogether, but in recent years there has been a revival of interest in managing coppice woodlands and utilising the products harvested.

- During the 20th century the area of coppice woodland declined from 230 000 ha to 23 000 ha.

- Not all woodlands or tree species are suitable for management as coppice: the system should only be used if it meets the management objectives for the woodland.

Further reading and references

ANDERSON, M.L. (1967).
A history of Scottish forestry, vols 1 and 2. Nelson, London.

ANON. (1928).
Report on census of woodlands and census of production of home-grown timber 1924. HMSO, London.
ANON. (1952).
Census of woodands 1947–1949. HMSO, London.
ANON. (1996).
Guidelines for identifying ancient woodland. English Nature, Peterborough.
BUCKLEY, G.P. (1992).
Ecology and management of coppice woodlands. Chapman and Hall, London.
CROWTHER, R.E. AND EVANS, J. (1986).
Coppice. Forestry Commission Leaflet 83. HMSO, London.
FERRIS, R. AND CARTER, C. (2000).
Managing rides, roadsides and edge habitats in lowland forests. Forestry Commission Bulletin 123. Forestry Commission, Edinburgh.
FORESTRY COMMISSION (1994).
The management of semi-natural woodlands. Forestry Commission Practice Guides 1–8. Forestry Commission, Edinburgh.
FULLER, R.J. AND WARREN, M.S. (1993).
Coppiced woodlands: their management for wildlife, 2nd edn. Joint Nature Conservation Committee, Peterborough.
HOWE, J. (1991).
Hazel coppice, 1st edn. Hampshire County Council, Winchester.
LINDSAY, J. M. (1975).
The history of oak coppice in Scotland. *Scottish Forestry* **29**, 87–93.
LINNARD, W. (2000).
Welsh woods and forests. Gomer, Llandysul.
LOCKE, G.M.L. (1970).
Census of woodlands 1965–67. HMSO, London.
LOCKE, G.M.L. (1987).
Census of woodlands and trees 1979–82. Forestry Commission Bulletin 63. HMSO, London.
MACPHERSON, G. (1995).
Home-grown energy from short-rotation coppice. Farming Press, Ipswich.
PETERKEN, G.F. (1996).
Natural woodland. Cambridge University Press, Cambridge.
RACKHAM, O. (1980).
Ancient woodland. Edward Arnold, London.
RODWELL, J.S. (1991).
British plant communities, vol. 1: *Woodlands and scrub.* Cambridge University Press, Cambridge.

SPENCER, J.W. AND KIRBY, K.J. (1992).

An inventory of ancient woodland for England and Wales. *Biological Conservation* **62**, 77–93.

TABOR, R. (1994).

Traditional woodland crafts. Batsford, London.

TUBBY, I. AND ARMSTRONG, A. (2002).

Establishment and management of short rotation coppice. Forestry Commission Practice Note 7 (revised). Forestry Commission, Edinburgh.

WATKINS, C. (1990).

Woodland management and conservation. David and Charles, Newton Abbot.

Mixed woodland of stored-coppice comprising stools of ash, field maple and oak with an understorey of hazel.

2. Coppice Silviculture

Coppice is a word that is used by foresters to cover many aspects of coppice systems including: a type of woodland consisting of trees that are periodically cut; the multi-stemmed trees that occur in such woodlands; the process of felling the trees; and the production of new shoots by the newly cut stools. Although the vocabulary associated with coppice silviculture is specialised, much of the old terminology which was probably regional in character, has fallen into disuse. For example more than 20 names have been recorded for standards including reserves, staddles, tellers and waverers; similarly the area of woodland cut in any year has had various names including sale, fell, cant and burrow.

The coppice system relies on the ability of trees to regrow from cut stumps and traditionally two systems of management were used in Britain: simple coppice and coppice with standards. A third system, uncommon in Britain, is the coppice selection system: although there are few records of this system being used, there is evidence to suggest that some woodlands were managed by this method (Coppins *et al.*, 2002). It is unlikely that all coppice woodlands were managed at all times as prescriptively as described below. The exact timing and amount of felling is likely to have responded to local requirements.

Simple coppice

This is an even-aged single storey crop grown for fuel wood and small/medium sized material. The coppice was cut on a regular rotation, the length of which depended not only on the product required but also on species, location, rate of growth and demand for materials. Theoretically the coppice was managed by sequential cutting of coupes throughout the woodland: ideally the length of the rotation was determined and the woodland divided into a number of coupes equal to the number of years in the rotation; one coupe was then cut each year. Coppice woodlands managed in this way, with coupes cut at the appropriate time in order to produce material of the desired size and quality, are said to be *in-cycle* or *in-rotation*. While such a regular system may have been possible, changes in demand or mis-management were likely to vary the process. Under current conditions a detailed systematic approach such as this is unlikely to be necessary unless there is a need for specialised crops; for example at present in some areas of the country there is a high demand for in-cycle hazel coppice to provide rods for hurdle making and these are best produced by regular cutting on a rotation of about 7 years.

Partially felled coupe of chestnut managed as simple coppice.

Coppice with standards

These woodlands are multi-storied with an even-aged lower storey of coppice underwood cut regularly to produce small material, and a partial overstorey of uneven-aged standard trees which are grown to produce large timber. This system is more difficult to manage than simple coppice as it is necessary to manage the number, age class distribution and location of large overstorey trees which affect the growth of the understorey crop.

The underwood is managed as simple coppice, but after cutting each coupe the number and age class distribution of standards present is adjusted: it is necessary to remove the oldest, reduce numbers of those of intermediate ages and recruit new standards.

Well-managed area of hazel coppice with oak standards. The overstorey canopy was reduced to about 15% and the site was temporarily fenced.

Coppice selection system

This method is similar to that for the selection system in high forests. Within the woods managed using this method the stools have populations of stems that are of both different size and age. A target diameter for the product is set, and the age at which the crop achieves this fixes the length of the rotation: this period is divided into a suitable number of felling cycles and the woodland area divided into a number of annual coupes which equals the number of years in the felling cycle (e.g. 30-year rotation, 3 felling cycles of 10 years, 10 annual coupes). Harvesting of stems that have reached the target diameter occurs annually within one of the coupes; all smaller stems remain uncut.

This is a special system that has been used with beech on poor ground in mountainous areas where the remaining canopy can have advantageous effects protecting both the new shoots and soil from damaging environmental factors such as frost, drought and erosion. However, due to the continuous canopy cover, the regrowth of shoots is poor relative to simple coppice, and harvesting the crop is difficult without damaging the smaller retained stems.

Recent experience in the management of ancient pollards (Read, 2000) suggests that old, neglected coppice stools, especially those of beech, may benefit from use of a modified form of selection coppice. Restoration occurs over a period of years with mature stems which are retained on stools at the first cut providing some protection from the damaging effects of strong, direct sunlight.

Current management

Many coppice woodlands have been left to grow substantially beyond the normal rotation and have developed stools with stems having the characteristic sizes and lengths of high forest trees. These are termed stored-coppice and although this implies a positive management decision it is often a euphemism for neglect (see Chapter 4). Extending the rotation of standards, allowing large trees to become more numerous, can have an adverse effect on the understorey (see Chapter 5).

Coppice is a good method by which woodlands can be managed to protect soils and habitats, and produce an uneven-aged canopy. In managed coppice that is well-stocked with stools, the regrowth of shoots after felling is rapid and the period in which there is no canopy cover is short in comparison to restocking from seedling trees. A range of ages and size classes will be produced by regular cutting of coupes within simple coppice, and also, by the overstory trees in coppice with standards.

Whilst there are well-defined, systematised methods for managing coppice woodlands they are unlikely to be of relevance in many of today's woodlands. In many instances management will involve the restoration of neglected or stored-coppice with further cutting taking place on an irregular basis over longer rotations than those traditionally used. On many sites, factors such as the control of felling coupe size, timing of rotation length and manipulating numbers of standards will be unimportant, but it will remain necessary to manage the woods carefully during the period of felling and regrowth to ensure that satisfactory restocking occurs.

Summary

• Two forms of coppice woodland are found in Britain: simple coppice which comprises coupes of even-aged coppice; and coppice with standards in which coupes comprise an understorey of even-aged coppice with an overstorey of uneven-aged standards.

Further reading and references

COPPINS, A., COPPINS, B. and QUELCH, P. (2002).
Atlantic hazel woods. *British Wildlife* **14**, 17–26.
JAMES, N.D.G (1981).
  A history of english forestry. Basil Blackwell, Oxford.
MASON, B., KERR, G. AND SIMPSON, J. (1999).
  What is continuous cover forestry? Forestry Commission Information Note 29.
  Forestry Commission, Edinburgh.
MATTHEWS, J.D. (1989).
  Silvicultural systems. Oxford University Press, Oxford.
PETERKEN, G.F. (1993).
  Woodland conservation and management, 2nd edn. Chapman and Hall, London.
READ, H. (2000).
  Veteran trees: a guide to good management. English Nature, Peterborough.

Expanding buds and shoots developing from suppressed buds on a stem of recently cut hazel.

3. Biology of Coppice Stools

The origins of coppice shoots

As shoots of broadleaved trees grow they produce lateral buds that are associated with both leaves and bud scales. Most of these newly formed buds are suppressed by the apical meristem and do not grow during the season in which they are formed: they become dormant and cannot form branches until they have been exposed to winter conditions that break their dormancy. The eventual fate of the lateral buds varies: on a typical temperate broadleaved tree some of those near the shoot tip will form branches; many will die and abscise; others, often the smallest, will remain suppressed and return to the dormant state growing slowly outwards as the stem increases in diameter. Throughout subsequent annual cycles of suppression/ dormancy/dormancy breaking during winter the suppressed buds remain poorly developed but they may divide to form large clusters of small buds embedded in the bark. These suppressed buds are the primary source not only of most coppice shoots but also the epicormic shoots which are a well-known problem of oak. When a stem is felled, the small buds, which are no longer suppressed by the tree's crown, can grow out to form new coppice shoots. The time of felling may have an influence on the timing of new shoot production, if stems are cut too late in the growing season when the suppressed buds have already become dormant, then new shoots are unlikely to form until the following season.

Coppice shoots may also grow from adventitious buds that develop from tissues not closely associated with suppressed buds. These adventitious buds are not formed as part of the normal developmental process and they often occur in callus formed in response to some form of wounding. Although many woody plants have the potential to form adventitious buds few are formed on stems. In contrast all buds which grow into suckers on roots are adventitious. When a tree stem is cut adventitious buds and coppice shoots can arise in the ring of callus that develops between the wood and the bark of the stump. Unlike suppressed buds most adventitious buds do not undergo a period of dormancy and they develop into shoots in the season in which they are formed. Whereas suppressed buds are connected to the vascular system via a vascular trace, adventitious buds and shoots must develop a new connection with the plant's vascular system. In North America this type of coppice shoot has been called a 'stool sprout' in order to distinguish it from a 'stump sprout' which develops from a suppressed bud. These 'stool sprouts' have been reported for several species including poplar, willow, elm, hornbeam, lime, horse chestnut, beech and sycamore. Adventitious coppice shoots are uncommon, short-lived and generally unimportant in the regeneration of most broadleaved trees.

The propensity for stems to regrow following coppicing varies with species, but it is also known that success depends on a number of other criteria which are both biological (e.g. age, size of stump, vigour of stems) and silvicultural (e.g. method and time of cutting, protection); these are discussed in the following sections.

Adventitious shoots developing from buds formed in the cambium on the stump remaining after felling a maiden beech.

Biological factors influencing the success of coppice

Age and size effects

The regrowth of cut stumps following felling is influenced by their age and diameter, but as these are usually related, their individual effects are difficult to disentangle. Most detailed studies of these factors have usually involved investigation of stumps from maiden trees (i.e. not previously coppiced) rather than multi-stemmed coppice stools that can have a complex structure comprising components with a variety of ages. For example, it is possible to have stools of similar age with stems of widely different sizes; in contrast stools can be of widely different ages yet have stems of similar sizes; and within a stool stems can vary in size and for some species also age (e.g. beech managed under a coppice selection system). In addition most of the studies have involved species that are not native to Britain (Table 3.1).

Table 3.1 Indicative list of species that have been studied to investigate the relationships between regrowth and the age or diameter of coppice stumps.

Oaks	
Quercus rubra	Quercus ilex
Quercus velutina	Quercus prinus
Quercus alba	Quercus stellata
Quercus coccinea	Quercus marilandica
Maples	
Acer saccharum	Acer rubrum
Birches	
Betula alleghaniensis	Betula pubescens
Betula papyrifera	Betula pendula
Others	
Liquidamber styraciflua	Nyssa aquatica
Alnus rubra	Nyssa sylvatica
Cornus florida	Prunus serotina

See Appendix for common names

Number and growth of coppice shoots

Despite the common occurrence of coppicing few species have been the subject of detailed study, and there is relatively little information concerning the number and growth of shoots after felling. Although Johnson (1977) has found that it is possible to predict the occurrence of co-dominant coppice stems on stumps of some North American oaks from their age, diameter and site quality, for most species it is not possible to give precise advice about the effect of either stump size, or age, on the probable number of shoots that will be produced and how they will grow. In general:

• There are relationships between stump diameter or age and number of shoots produced and their initial height and diameter growth.

• There are differences between species.

• For 'small' stumps there is a positive relationship between stump diameter and both number of shoots produced and their growth; in contrast, for 'large' diameter stumps there is a negative relationship between growth and numbers of shoots (i.e. for 'small' stumps more shoots are produced as diameter increases, but for 'large' stumps fewer shoots are produced as diameter increases). The critical stump size at which the change between positive and negative relationships occur varies with species and site.

• Both the number and growth of shoots tend to decline with stump age, but the age at which this becomes significant varies with species and site.

Mortality of stumps

Whilst shoot numbers and their growth are important factors to consider during management of stools, particularly for those who may be interested in yield, they are secondary to ensuring stool survival which may be of major importance for the maintenance of the mixture, abundance and genotype of species within semi-natural woodlands. Although there are data from a wide range of species it is still only possible to give broad advice on mortality which is similar to that for shoot number and growth. In general, the mortality of stumps tends to increase with both age and size, but the relationships vary with species.

The variability both between species, and between sites for the same species, is probably due, in part, to the vigour of the parent stem, for example:

- Regrowth from *Acer rubrum* stumps up to 40 cm in diameter is influenced by 10 year average basal area increment (Solomon and Blum, 1967).

- The differences in mortality of 4 species of oak is related to the initial average height of the species in the stand (Little, 1938).

- Shoots are more numerous and grow better from stools of *Quercus ilex* that initially have larger and more numerous stems (Ducrey and Turrel, 1992).

- For *Castanea dentata* the optimum age for sprouting coincides with the period of maximum height growth, about 20–30 years old (Mattoon, 1909).

Site quality may influence the success of coppicing by its effect on vigour with slow growing stools on poor sites regrowing less well than those on good sites. In general, whatever their age or size, poorly growing or suppressed stools and stems in neglected stands, will respond less favourably to coppicing than those which are growing vigorously.

Several suggestions have been made to explain the decline in shoot numbers and survival of stumps as they become older or larger and these may be related to: the loss of viable dormant buds from the stem either due to age or reduced vigour; the presence of a thick bark which restricts the growth of deeply embedded buds; and changes which occur when the trees reach the age at which they flower. However, none of these have been adequately studied.

Silvicultural factors influencing the success of coppicing

Seasonal effects

The time of cutting has been shown to influence regrowth of a variety of species, and whilst there is some variation, it has generally been found that stem survival, and initial numbers and growth of new shoots is usually better when trees are cut during the dormant season between late autumn and early spring. In subsequent years the initial differences in numbers and growth of shoots may disappear. If shoots are produced after a summer cut then winter damage may be more severe than for those produced early in the season due to insufficient growth and hardening-off. Data for coppicing of young maiden trees growing in southern Britain are given in Figures 3.1 and 3.2.

Figure 3.1

Mean height (cm) of the 3 longest coppice shoots on stumps of 6-year-old maiden tree stems that were cut in February, April and June 1993: heights were measured at the end of each growing season for 6 years. For oak, the shoots regrowing after the June cut were always shortest, but those of sycamore and ash attained similar heights to the dormant season treatments after 3 and 6 years respectively.

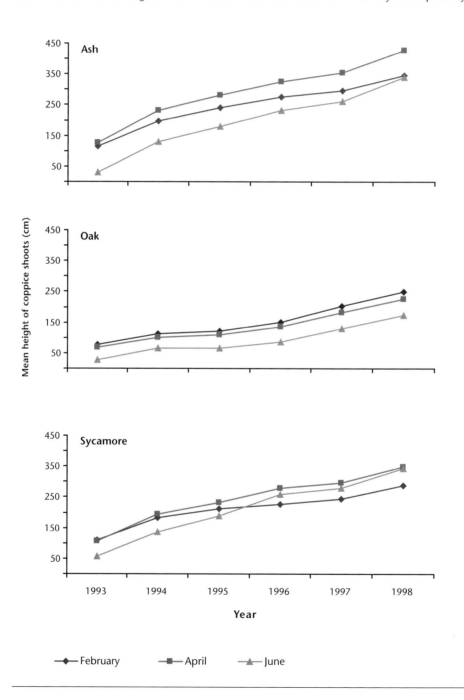

Figure 3.2

Mean number of coppice shoots after 1 and 6 seasons growth on stumps of 6-year-old maidens of ash, oak and sycamore felled in February, April and June 1993. Total heights of bars are the mean number of shoots at end of the first season; shaded areas are the number after 6 seasons. For all species at all felling dates the number of shoots declined markedly during the first 6 years of growth.

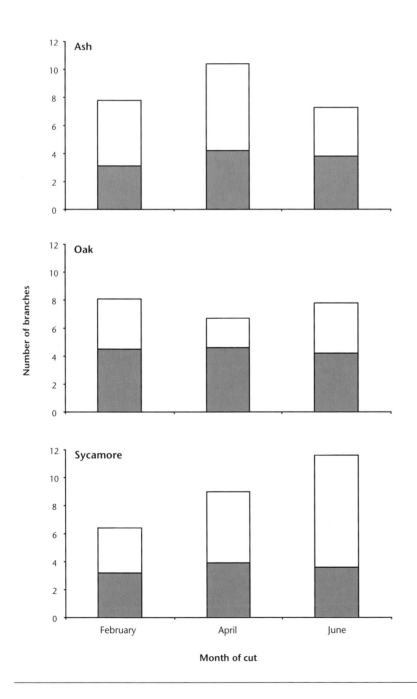

Height of the stump

The position of the cut and size of the stem remaining can influence subsequent growth but effects may vary with species and time.

The initial number of shoots produced by some species increases with stump height (Table 3.2), but differences may decline with time, and for some species may not occur. For some species low cut stumps may suffer greater mortality than those which are cut high (Table 3.3).

Table 3.2 Number of coppice shoots present after 1 and 6 seasons' growth on stumps of 6-year-old maidens cut in early spring 1993

Species	Growth (years)	Height of cut above ground	
		5 cm	15 cm
Ash	1	6.8	11.5
	6	3.4	4.0
Beech	1	2.0	4.1
	6	2.5	3.2
Oak	1	5.3	7.4
	6	3.5	4.3
Sycamore	1	3.9	7.8
	6	2.7	3.5

Table 3.3 Effect of stump height on the percentage of mountain maple, paper birch and pin cherry stumps with sprouts after two growing seasons (Jobidon, 1997)

Species	Stump height (cm)			
	0	15	45	75
Mountain maple	31	22	37	71
Paper birch	35	18	33	73
Pin cherry	69	38	79	89

When stumps are cut high the probability of butt rot occurring in the stems that develop is increased. This can have consequences for both the quality of stems in stored coppice (Table 3.4) and the longevity of the stool which will rot in the centre and may become unstable if neglected.

Table 3.4 Percentage of coppice stems with butt rot 32 years after felling maiden trees of 3 species leaving stumps of different height (data adapted from Roth and Hepting, 1969)

Stump height[a]	Tall		Short	
Shoot origin[b]	Low	High	Low	High
White oak	21	38	3	0
Black oak	12	32	17	14
Scarlet oak	9	44	0	-

[a] Tall = stumps 30 cm tall; short = stumps cut at or near ground level.
[b] Height from which coppice shoot originates: low = less than 2.5 cm above ground level; high = greater than 2.5 cm above ground level.

On some species, the shoots that arise on high cut stumps develop from buds in areas of thick bark which constricts development of their vascular connection with the stump. Although the base of the branch grows in diameter the joint between the branch and stump is unstable.

Cutting close to the ground will encourage new shoots to grow near to or below ground level and allow them to develop their own root system.

Coppice species in Britain

Although it is well known that many trees occurring in Britain can be regenerated by coppicing (e.g. Rackham, 1990) there is a dearth of detailed information on these species, but they probably show similar characteristics to those growing elsewhere. The information in Table 3.5 summarises data collected from a survey of sites in southern England which was made in order to indicate how stools respond to coppicing. The survey was made at 49 sites and the table shows information on survival and regrowth that was collected 2–3 years after cutting. Stools of 19 different species were found, some such as ash, birch and hazel being present at more than 20 sites. There was wide variation in the number of stools of each species that were observed, with hazel being most frequent. In general less than 10% of the stools had died after coppicing. For all species except blackthorn and wild cherry there was great variation in the length of the longest shoot produced by each stool, for example the average length of the longest coppice shoot produced by field maple was 2100 mm, but this varied between a minimum of 280 mm and a maximum of 3500 mm. For most species less than 90% of the shoots had grown more than the 1200 mm needed to escape browsing by roe and muntjac deer; fewer had grown more than the 1800 mm needed to escape fallow deer. Further information on browsing is given in Chapter 6.

Table 3.5 Regrowth of coppice stools in southern England 2–3 years after cutting

Species	Sites	Stools		Longest shoot		
		Number	% dead	Mean (min–max)	>1200 mm	>1800 mm
Ash	27	304	11	1600 (30–4200)	57	49
Alder	2	85	32	1650 (440–2900)	85	29
Aspen	1	6	0	330 (120–600)	0	0
Beech	8	32	16	540 (30–1630)	19	0
Birch	27	191	35	1780 (30–4500)	62	51
Elder	3	6	0	1980 (470–2800)	83	50
Field maple	10	51	0	2100 (280–3500)	94	69
Hazel	37	860	5	2050 (40–4250)	85	66
Hornbeam	6	243	9	2260 (50–4200)	88	80
Hawthorn	13	66	12	1130 (60–3500)	40	8
Holly	9	30	3	440 (50–1490)	3	0
Lime	2	50	0	1820 (900–3000)	88	44
Oak	19	220	25	1060 (30–2490)	42	14
Rowan	4	10	0	1120 (310–4050)	20	20
Sweet chestnut	7	131	4	2860 (110–5990)	92	84
Blackthorn	2	2	0	1500 (1490–1500)	100	0
Sycamore	11	92	2	1600 (50–4000)	62	32
Wild cherry	1	1	0	2100 (2100–2100)	100	100
Willow	11	44	7	1840 (70–3820)	63	59

Data are combined results over all sites.
Sites = number of sites where species was present.
Number = number of stools observed.
% Dead = percentage of stools that were dead.
Mean = average length of longest shoot on stools; (min-max) = minimum and maximum lengths of longest shoots on stools;
>1200 = percentage of longest shoots that were longer than 1200 mm; >1800 = percentage of longest shoots that were longer than 1800 mm.

Longevity of stools

The life span of a stool will depend on a variety of factors including species, environment and management; good growing conditions where soils are fertile, the climate is favourable and overstorey canopy cover is low will enhance longevity of the stools. Those that are cut on a regular rotation, when stems are young and of small diameter, will survive longer than those that are cut on less regular, long rotations. Failure to prevent excessive browsing can have severe effects on the survival of stools. Neglected stools can survive for many years with stems attaining large dimensions but their ability to regrow after cutting will decline with age. Species will vary but the longevity of a neglected stool will be related to its quality (e.g. age, size and vigour) and structure (small, old, suppressed stools which are rotting will not survive as well as those that are healthy, vigorous and young). Whilst the age of coppice stools can be estimated from their dimensions much of the information on the longevity of worked coppice stools is probably based on casual observation and anecdote.

Ancient hornbeam coppice woodland with many large, old stools.

Summary

• Although coppice shoots can arise from adventitious buds most grow from dormant suppressed buds.

• Most detailed knowledge about regrowth of coppice has been obtained by study of maiden stumps, little of the information has been collected from British species.

• Species differ in their response to coppicing.

• The effects of stump age, size and site are difficult to disentangle.

• The number and growth of shoots tend to decline with stump age but relationships with diameter vary with age.

• Stump mortality tends to increase with age and diameter. Stool longevity depends on tree biology, environment and stool management.

• Poorly growing stools will respond less well to coppicing than those growing vigorously.

• Felling is probably best carried out in the dormant season.

Further reading and references

BLAKE, T.J. (1983).
  Coppice systems for short rotation intensive forestry: the influence of cultural, seasonal and plant factors. *Australian Forest Research* **13**, 279–291.
BÜSGEN, M., MÜNCH, E. AND THOMPSON, T. (1929).
  The structure and life of forest trees. Chapman and Hall, London.
CLARK, F.B. AND LIMING, F.G. (1953).
  Sprouting of blackjack oak in the Missouri Ozarks. USDA Forest Service Central States Forest Experimental Station Technical Paper 137. USDA, Columbia, Missouri.
DEL TREDICI, P. (2001).
  Sprouting in temperate trees: a morphological and ecological review. *Botanical Review* **67**, 121–140.
DUCREY, M. AND TURREL, M. (1992).
  Influence of cutting methods and dates on stump sprouting in holm oak (*Quercus ilex* L.) coppice. *Annales Sciences Forestiere* **49**, 449–464.

JOBIDAN, R. (1997).
  Stump height effects on sprouting of mountain maple, paper birch and pin cherry
  – 10 year results. *The Forestry Chronicle* **73**, 590–595.
JOHNSON, P.S. (1977).
  Predicting oak stump sprouting and sprout development in the Missouri Ozarks.
  USDA Forest Service Research Paper NG 149. St Paul, Minnesota.
KRAMER, P.S. AND KOZLOWSKII, T.T. (1979).
  Physiology of woody plants. Academic Press, New York.
LITTLE, S. (1938).
  Relationships between vigor of resprouting and intensity of cutting in coppice
  stands. *Journal of Forestry* **36**, 1216–1223.
MATTOON, W.R. (1909).
  The origin and early development of chestnut sprouts. *Forestry Quarterly* **7**, 34–47.
RACKHAM, O. (1990).
  Trees and woodlands in the British landscape. J. M. Dent and Sons Ltd, London.
ROTH, E.R. AND HEPTING, G.H. (1969).
  Prediction of butt rot in newly regenerated sprout oak stands. *Journal of Forestry*
  67, 756–760.
SCHLICH, W. (1910).
  Schlich's manual of forestry, vol. II: *Silviculture,* 4th edn. Bradbury Agnew and
  Co Ltd, London.
SOLOMON, D.S. AND BLUM, B.M. (1967).
  Stump sprouting in four northern hardwoods. USDA Forest Service Research
  Paper NE–59. USDA, Upper Darby, Pennsylvania.
ZIMMERMANN, M.H. AND BROWN, C.L. (1971).
  Trees structure and function. Springer-Verlag, Berlin.
SMITH, D.M. (1986).
  The practice of silviculture, 8th edn. John Wiley & Sons, New York.

Extracting from a recently felled coupe of neglected mixed broadleaved coppice which had not been cut for about 60 years. The yield was about 240 tonnes ha^{-1}.

4. Practical Aspects of Management

Before embarking on woodland management using coppice it is necessary to decide whether the system will achieve the objectives of management in both the short and the long term: it should not be assumed that woodlands that were previously coppiced could, or should, continue to be managed in a similar way.

In order to decide whether coppice is appropriate it is necessary to assess the site carefully observing factors such as: quality, number and vigour of stools; size, distribution and species of standards; and presence of damaging animals. After this it will be necessary to estimate how well the stools and woodland will respond to treatment and whether they can be managed appropriately to maximise the possibility of success. It is particularly important to consider how excessive herbivore damage will be prevented.

The following sections describe some of the practical aspects of managing stools that may influence success and the decision on whether coppice is appropriate. It must be remembered that:

- all woodlands are different;
- stools will vary both within and between species;
- stems within a stool may each benefit from their own special treatment.

Felling 50-year-old stems of neglected hazel coppice.

Felling Licences

A Felling Licence from the Forestry Commission is normally required to fell growing trees but in any calendar quarter up to 5 cubic metres may be felled without a licence provided that no more than 2 cubic metres are sold. If this quota is exceeded then the owner, timber merchant and feller may all be liable to prosecution.

There are certain exceptions, including the following, that are most relevant to the management of coppice woodlands:

• Approval under a Forestry Commission Grant Scheme.

• If the stems are coppice or underwood with a diameter ≤ 15 cm at a height of 1.3 m above ground (dbh).

• If the felling is a thinning operation and all stems are ≤ 10 cm dbh.

• All trees are ≤ 8 cm dbh.

Full details can be obtained from Forestry Commission offices.

Management of stools

Method of cutting

Traditionally coppice was cut using hand tools and since chainsaws were introduced there have been a number of trials to investigate whether there are any differences in growth after cutting with different tools. No differences of any practical significance have been found and in most cases the question is irrelevant as the stools are frequently neglected and have large diameter stems, and a chainsaw is the only realistic option.

The quality of the cut is more important than the tool used: it is important that cuts are clean with no separation of the bark from the wood on the stool that remains.

The choice of tool depends on the skill, training and preference of the worker, the size of the coppice shoots, and the ease with which tools can be used: for the experienced woodman working in-cycle hazel coppice the bilhook remains the most effective tool for cutting and preparing rods; a bow saw is probably the most appropriate tool for unskilled workers cutting small diameter stems; large diameter stems on neglected stools are best cut by trained staff using chainsaws.

Coppice worker using a billhook to cut small chestnut stems for use as walking sticks.

Bundles of trimmed chestnut stems awaiting collection prior to export to Germany.

Type of cut

Old literature suggests that shoots should be cut to ensure that water drains from the centre of the stool, the cut surface of the stump should have a sloping face to shed water, and be south-facing to dry more quickly. There is little quantitative evidence to support this logical suggestion but young, maiden red alder stumps with a flat surface showed greater mortality than those with cut surfaces having southerly or westerly aspects (Table 4.1). Comparisons of flat and south-sloping cuts on young oak, ash, beech and sycamore in Alice Holt Forest found no relationship between type of cut and either mortality, shoot numbers or height growth (Table 4.2).

Table 4.1 Percentage mortality of red alder in relation to aspect of the cut surface (Harrington, 1984)

Age class (years)	Aspect			
	Flat	N/NE	E, SE, NW	S, SW, W
1–5	25	21	15	12
6–16	59	33	44	27

Table 4.2 Percentage of live stumps and height of longest shoot after 6 seasons of growth from maidens cut at 15 cm above ground with either flat or south-facing surfaces sloping at 45 degrees

Species	Flat		Sloping	
	%	Height (cm)	%	Height (cm)
Ash	97	236	100	226
Beech	65	221	70	213
Oak	94	292	97	280
Sycamore	100	322	100	339

Although the structure of many coppice stools will make it difficult to fell stems leaving a cut surface with a generally southerly aspect, all should be clean and sloping, wherever possible, towards the outside of the stool.

Position of cut

In order to encourage the development of new shoots at or below ground level, promote root development, reduce butt rot and increase the stability of the shoot system, maintain the stool at a level close to the ground.

When felling maiden stumps cut as close to the ground as possible unless the site is subject to flooding when higher cuts may be appropriate. On established stools it is generally inadvisable to cut into old wood below the level of the last cut; fell close to the height of the last cut leaving short stumps.

It is possible to restrict the amount of browsing damage due to deer by cutting stems at 1.2 m or higher but this can have adverse effects on the structure and stability of the stool, and make safe working difficult when further harvests are made. Such stools could be regarded as short pollards and may subsequently require different management.

Ancient stool of ash that has been cut many times and rotted in its centre.

New shoots growing on the stump remaining after felling hornbeam at a height of about 1.3 m above ground in an attempt to reduce browsing damage.

Time of cutting

The best time to cut coppice is during the dormant winter period: the bark is less likely to tear from the wood; stump mortality will probably be reduced; and new shoots are likely to grow better and suffer less frost/winter damage than shoots formed after a summer cut. The absence of foliage will make working easier.

Although winter cutting may also have some conservation benefits, such as causing no disturbance to nesting birds and reduced direct damage to the ground flora, the moisture content of soils will be high and they will be more readily damaged than during the drier conditions which occur in summer. Operations should be carried out in accordance with nature and soil conservation guidelines.

Restocking and restoration of coppice

It is inevitable that stools will die and numbers decline to a level at which the quality of the coppice will be threatened. Prior to any management it will be necessary to evaluate the site and decide if current stool densities are sufficient or whether restocking is required. The stool density necessary will depend on a variety of factors including whether the site is to be retained as coppice, converted to high forest, the yield of product required and the species present.

Retention as coppice

The density of stools required for in-cycle, productive, traditional coppice depends on the crop required, with density declining as size of product and rotation increase: hazel on short rotations of 6–12 years may have 1250–2000 ha^{-1}; sweet chestnut with a rotation length of 12–16 years 800–1000 ha^{-1}; and oak rotation on 20+ years only a few hundred. Exact numbers will vary with vigour of the crop and size of stool, but there must be sufficient stools present to provide complete canopy cover across the site within a few years of cutting. Low stool densities will not only reduce yield, but for hazel will also influence the quality of the crop, with those stools in poorly stocked areas producing wide spreading, bushy crowns with curved, branched stems.

In woodlands managed on more irregular coppice cycles, or for conservation or amenity objectives, the stool density in relation to yield and quality will have less relevance. However it must be considered as other related changes are inevitable, for example, where stool density declines and the canopy thins, the ground flora will change and shade tolerant weedy species such as bramble increase in abundance. This may have beneficial effects for some animals but adverse effects on some plants.

Where there are insufficient stools then restocking should take place or an alternative form of woodland management be considered. The decision to restock with new stools depends on the objectives of management; if the current stool density will not allow these to be achieved then restocking must take place regardless of objective. For example a site managed for the quality of its flora under a traditional hazel coppice system is unlikely to retain its interest if stool densities and canopy cover decline; similarly a good crop of hazel coppice is unlikely unless there are sufficient stools to produce at least 25 000 rods ha[-1] (Table 4.3).

Table 4.3 Number of usable rods[a] per stool needed in hazel crops with different stool densities to achieve different quality grades

Stool density (ha[-1])	Grade 1	Grade 2	Grade 3
1000	30	20	10
1375	22	15	8
1875	16	11	5

[a]A rod is a stem which has a minimum usable length of 2.5 m but may be up to 5 m, with a basal diameter in the region of 1.5–5 cm. Data adapted from Wessex coppice group guidance.

Conversion to high forest

Throughout the past 50–100 years many woods which were traditionally managed as coppice have developed a high forest structure following growth after the cessation of regular cutting. These crops, which comprise trees known as stored-coppice, are simple to produce but may not be appropriate for all sites or species, and the decision to use the method may only delay the problem of restocking until a future date. This is the situation that currently affects many neglected woodlands with overmature coppice stems on old coppice stools which, if cut, may neither survive nor produce a suitable crop for the future.

Stored-coppice trees

Although storing coppice is a simple procedure it has a number of drawbacks which may influence the decision on whether or not it should be used. In comparison with maidens of the same species, growth may be inferior, the stems be of worse form with more butt sweep, and the inclusion of wood from the old stool may cause stem defects. The trees produced are often less stable than maidens which may cause problems of windthrow after subsequent felling operations. In addition the method cannot be used on areas dominated by hazel which does not develop into a high forest canopy tree.

During the years following cutting the number of shoots on coppice stools reduces by natural processes, but silvicultural thinning to reduce stem number during the second half of the rotation has been recommended to improve the quality of sweet chestnut poles and oak stems for tan bark. Similarly, the quality of stored-coppice can be improved by 'singling' to remove from the stool all stems except that which is judged to be the straightest and most vigorous. Subsequent thinning of the stand would be similar to that for plantation forests. Under such a regime the cut stools remaining after thinning are likely to be suppressed and die: this will restrict the opportunity to revert easily to a traditional coppice system.

If the objective is to convert to high forest then this method of treating coppice should be regarded as an interim measure prior to the establishment of single stemmed trees by planting or natural regeneration. It is likely to be most successful where stools are young, vigorous, have been cut close to the ground and are free from decay. It has the advantage of retaining tree cover, is relatively cheap and crop trees do not need repeated protection from browsing animals.

Neglected woodlands

The management decisions in these woods can only be made after a careful assessment of the site. The distribution, density and identity of stools and standards across the site must be observed in order to discover if there are sufficient of those species capable of forming a high forest. Stool quality must be assessed in order to determine whether each will survive and grow to produce a canopy tree of sufficiently high quality to meet the objectives of management. As neglected stools are often prone to wind damage, felling operations during any process of restoration, conversion or restocking should minimise any risks: clear cutting small coupes may be inappropriate and thinning over a long period may be necessary. There will be differences both between and within sites in the treatments needed to achieve success: some areas may be suitably managed using existing stools but others may need restocking.

Methods of restocking

There are three methods that should be considered: vegetative propagation from existing stools; natural regeneration from seed; and transplanting of nursery-grown seedlings. Which of these is appropriate will depend on a variety of factors including species present, site type, silvicultural history and future objectives of management. Their usefulness will vary both between and within sites.

Vegetative propagation

The ability of plants to produce adventitious roots on shoots is the basis of the process of layering that is a traditional method of filling gaps where stools have died. It is a procedure which works well with species such as alder, ash, chestnut, hazel, lime and willow.

There are several methods by which layering can be carried out, the simplest of which are described briefly below.

Simple layering

This is probably best carried out in the autumn or late winter/early spring when parent shoots from the mother plant are arched over and pegged down to the soil. To improve rooting the shoot can be wounded about 30 cm from the tip: this can be done by sharply twisting using both hands or cutting halfway through the stem for a length of 25–50 mm using a knife. The shoots should be pegged down into a shallow (*c.* 10 cm) scrape where the wound was made and then covered with soil.

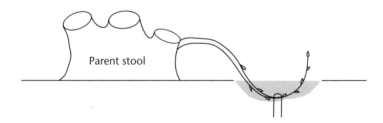

Parent stool

Trench layering

During winter, before bud break begins, parent shoots should be pegged down flat (not arched) into a trench about 5 cm deep and 25 cm wide, and then covered with soil. Any lateral branches should be pruned to enable burial of the shoot within the trench.

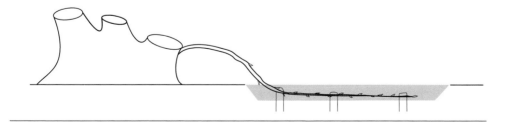

Stooling

This is a very simple method by which earth is mounded over a stool on one or more occasions during spring and early summer to a total depth of 30 cm. This will encourage roots to develop on shoots without the need for laying and pegging parent shoots.

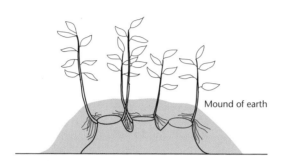

Mound of earth

Traditionally layering was carried out after a coppice cut using shoots 2.5–5.0 cm basal diameter that were left on the stool. If shoots of this size are used then a cut about half-way through the stem, near the base, may be necessary to enable pegging of larger diameter shoots. Whilst use of these old shoots will take advantage of the good light and weed-free conditions occurring after a cut, they may not root as well as young shoots grown on a recently cut stool. Horticultural practice recommends using shoots 1 or 2 years old for simple and trench layering, and current year shoots that are a few weeks old for stooling.

Adequate weed control will be necessary during the period in which the layers establish. A single stool can be used to produce many layers which can be transplanted after 2–3 years when they are well rooted.

Whilst layering is simple it requires special skills and experience to carry out the process and maintain the plants during propagation. It may not be suitable for all sites, for example, where it is too dark. If it is used as a method of plant production and the layers are dug up and transplanted, then careful management, record keeping and planning are required. It will be difficult to achieve on sites with little regular management input, and where there is no permanent manager, woodman or other staff. Although it conserves existing local genotypes it does not allow a change of species, which may be necessary on some sites where more diversity or a change of silvicultural system is wanted, e.g. if converting from a site dominated by hazel to one with a more high forest character.

Natural regeneration

Current policy and guidance prefer the use of natural regeneration for restocking in semi-natural woodlands, and whilst this method should be used wherever possible it can be difficult to achieve on some sites. Before choosing this option it is necessary to consider a number of factors including:

- Is there any existing evidence that natural regeneration will occur on this site, e.g. are any seedlings already present?

- What seed trees are present, are they the species that are wanted and will they produce enough seed when it is required?

- Where are the parent trees located and will the seed disperse to the areas where it is needed?

- Are the site conditions suitable for seeds to germinate and trees to establish. How will site conditions change during any procedure to stimulate natural regeneration. What management will be needed to promote success?

Naturally regenerating oak seedlings within a fenced area of oak coppice in the Wyre Forest. The soils are infertile and acidic, and the competition from the ground flora is relatively weak. The tallest stems in the middle are oak coppice shoots infected with mildew.

Within woodland the most successful natural regeneration is likely to occur where a dense canopy has strongly suppressed the ground flora. In coppice woodland such areas will probably have high stool densities, and restocking will be unnecessary unless the stools are very old and unlikely to survive felling, or a change of species or conversion to high forest wanted. In contrast, those areas of poor, understocked coppice where canopies are thin and broken, which are most in need of restocking, are the areas where natural regeneration is most difficult to achieve due to the presence of a well-developed ground flora of competitive weedy species. In these circumstances significant management input may be required if restocking by natural regeneration is to succeed.

Planting

This is a well-established procedure that is probably the most effective method of ensuring successful restocking. Planting allows great flexibility and can be used to change species composition, replace poor quality stools during conversion to high forest, and restock both large and small areas. In semi-natural woodlands planting stock should preferably be of local origin. Although practical problems of planting are well understood, and suitable methods exist for establishing trees on a wide variety of site types, all sites should be assessed to decide whether planting is appropriate and, if so, how planted trees should be managed. Routine prescriptions are not always appropriate. The vigorous growth from newly cut stools will provide significant competition to transplants, and when gapping-up or enrichment planting within well-stocked coppice areas robust transplants 0.5 m tall with root collar diameters of 5.5–9.5 mm and good quantities of intact healthy roots should be used (Table 4.4).

Table 4.4 Minimum root collar diameters for robust transplants 0.5 m tall

Species	Root collar diameter (mm)
Common alder	7.5
Ash	9.5
Beech	7.5
Birch	5.5
Sweet chestnut	9.5
Lime	9.5
Oak	9.5

Data from British Standard BS 3936 (Part 4).

Vigorous regrowth from ash stumps 3 years after felling 6-year-old maidens.

On sites where competion is likely to be very severe then even larger transplants may be appropriate. In contrast, on areas where cover from existing coppice and standards is sparse and competition from other vegetation low then smaller transplants may be acceptable. If tree shelters are necessary then they should be made of clear or white plastic to allow maximum light transmission.

When restocking to form new stools the newly planted trees should not be cut until they are well established and have been growing for several years.

In order to maximise the chances of success then the guidance and best practice described in the Further Reading list should be followed. The relative merits of some aspects of each restocking method are compared in Table 4.5. Whatever methods are used to restock with new plants, for management either as coppice stools or maidens in high forest, it is necessary to take adequate precautions to protect small young plants from browsing animals.

Harvesting damage

As the next crop develops from the crop which is being harvested careful planning and practice are needed in order to avoid unnecessary damage to both stools and standards. When establishing new coppice coupes they should be arranged to allow the extraction of produce from a recently felled coupe without the need to pass through other coupes. Ideally there should be a good system of internal roads and rides servicing each coupe, removing the need to extract through standing crops. Good permanent access is essential if coppice is to be managed on a regular basis. Avoid damage to stools when driving machinery or using other equipment on site. All produce should be removed before flushing begins in order to avoid damage to new shoots.

Table 4.5 Some characteristics of vegetative propagation, natural regeneration and planting for restoring coppice

Factor(s)	Layering	Natural regeneration	Planting
Biodiversity and Conservation	Maintains local geno-types by clonal propagation but may restrict genetic variation.	Maintains local genotypes by germination of seed *in situ*.	Local genotypes can be maintained by using nursery stock grown from locally collected seed.
		Matches species to appropriate microhabitats across the site.	Careful choice of planting site can match species to appropriate microhabitat.
		Produces woodland with greater structural diversity.	Innovative planting designs can produce woodlands with diverse structure.
Procedure	Technical procedure requiring horticultural skills, also needs specialist management during propagation period.	Managers and contractors often have little detailed knowledge or practical ex-perience of the process, re-quires ecological awareness.	Level of knowledge and experience generally high amongst all involved in the process.
	Two phase process comprising propagation and transplanting both of which require care and attention to detail.	High level of detail required in site assessment and development of a site specific management plan.	Broad, generalised prescriptions can be used on many sites.
	Flexible approach needed to apply formal methods.	Flexible approach to management necessary at all stages.	Procedures can be more formalised but must still respond adequately to changing site conditions.
	Labour intensive procedure only useful on small scale.	On some favourable sites may be cheaper than planting, but the cost of achieving success is initially unknown.	The cost of successful establishment can be predicted with reasonable accuracy before work begins.
Silviculture	Can have unpredictable results.	Probability of success low or unpredictable on some sites.	Predictability of success generally high.
	Direct control over species but choice restricted entirely to those present on site.	The diversity and abundance of species that develop on the site are difficult to control and derive initially from those in the immediate locality.	The species planted and proportions of each can be clearly defined.
	Can be used instead of planting.	Can supplement planting	Can be used to enrich natural regeneration
	Weed control may be a problem during propagation and establishment of transplanted layers.	If weed control becomes necessary, it may be difficult in randomly distributed plants of different sizes.	Where the location of plants is known, then weed control is easy to carry out.

Damage caused during extraction has removed much of the bark from this stool. The emerging coppice shoots have been browsed.

If lop and top is burnt to clear the coupe then as few fire sites as possible should be used; guidance by Mummery and Tabor (1978) for woodlands in Essex suggests that 20 per hectare should be enough, although the 6–8 per hectare suggested by Watkins (1990) is probably more appropriate especially in areas of high conservation value. Restrict damage to stools by locating fire sites in sparsely stocked areas that are well away from standards. Reuse the same fires sites whenever possible during future operations.

Standard (left) and hazel stools (right) damaged by inappropriate location of fire sites.

Yield from coppice woods

The length of coppice rotations were traditionally determined by the size of the end product required rather than the necessity to maximise productivity, and detailed information on the yield from coppice woodlands is scarce. Whilst there are provisional yield tables for hazel, oak and sweet chestnut coppice (Jeffers, 1956; Crockford and Savill, 1991; Rollinson and Evans, 1987) there is only limited information for other species.

Estimation of yield from low value, mixed broadleaved coppice woods is probably best achieved by using an abbreviated tariff method as described (Edwards, 1983). The recommended method is Step 1 method B with Step 2 method 5. This involves the laying out and measurement of sample plots. Sample plot sizes should be sufficient to represent the variation encountered in coppice woodlands. The number of plots will depend on the area and uniformity of the stand as shown in Table 4.6. As the stools in coppice woodlands often vary in size, quality and species it is recommended that the number of plots should not be less than the number of plots required for variable stands.

Each species in the plot should be treated separately, as follows. Measure the diameter of each stem with a breast height diameter (dbh) ≥ 7 cm, on every stool in every plot. Within each plot, select at random two sample stems with a dbh ≥ 10 cm and measure their timber height. Obtain tariff numbers for each sample stem from the appropriate species single tree tariff chart (Hamilton, 1998). Calculate the average tariff number for all the sample stems and calculate the volume for the species. These volume estimates may be expensive to obtain relative to the value of the stand. To reduce costs the area can be stratified on the basis of species productivity with an abbreviated tariff carried out for the most productive species only. For the less productive species roughly estimate the volume for a small representative area and apply to the whole area.

Actual yields from five coppice sites dominated by a variety of species are shown in Table 4.7; for most species these are probably lower than would be expected from well-managed, fully stocked, in-cycle coppice. Estimates of likely yields have been made and Insley (1988) suggested that for oak on 20–35-year rotations these are 3–7 m^3 ha^{-1} yr^{-1}, and for ash, sycamore and other hardwoods or mixed coppice on 20–25-year rotations 6–10 m^3 ha^{-1} yr^{-1}.

Table 4.6 Number of sample plots recommended for different areas and uniformity of coppice

Area of stand (ha)	Uniform stand	Variable stand
0.5–2.0	6	8
2–10	8	12
>10	10	16

Table 4.7 Yields from some species of coppice (adapted from Begley and Coates, 1961)

Species	Soil type	Number of stems ha⁻¹		Stools ha⁻¹	Maidens ha⁻¹	Age (yr)	Top height (m)	Yield (fresh weight tonnes ha⁻¹)		MAI (m³ ha⁻¹ yr⁻¹)
		≤5 cm	>5 cm					≥8.75 cm	≥5 cm	
Site 1										
Sycamore	Sandy loam	1275	2500	475	50	16	12.3	47	67	
English elm				75	50					
Birch				50	100					
Site 2										
Ash	Gleyed calcareous clay	200	2125	600	100	32	15	75	94	2.8
Birch				-	225					
Ash	Gleyed calcareous clay	500	2300	600	450	32	13.5	102	126	3.8
Birch				-	50					
Site 3										
Lime	Clay	975	2450	375	-	12	9.2	34	49	3.5
Lime		1325	3450	370	-	12	9.5	42	64	4.2
Site 4										
Oak	Sandy loam	350	1575	425	50	37	12.6	190	216	5.1
Sweet chestnut				-	50					
Birch				-	50					
Oak	Sandy loam	200	1425	400	25	37	13.8	155	158	3.6
Wild cherry				-	25					
Site 5										
Alder	Alkaline peat	1425	3825	625	-	20	9.9	66	88	4.0
Birch				50	-					
Willow				25	-					
Alder	Alkaline peat	1450	3850	450	-	20	11.4	96	138	5.8
Birch				-	25					
Willow				25	25					

Only oak was previously managed as coppice, for other coppice stools the stems are first growth from maiden stems. Yield includes maiden trees. Data for each species are for different plots on the same site. Species in bold type are the predominant species of coppice. MAI: mean annual increment.

Uses and markets for coppice

Although increased industrialisation, use of coal and other sources of energy and conversion of woodland to farmland has caused a large decline in the area of coppice woodland there has in recent years been a revival of interest in managing coppice woodland. Whilst this may often be for conservation purposes well-managed crops of some species can be profitable although this may depend on local markets to reduce transport costs.

In previous centuries raw materials from coppice woodlands have been used for a wide variety of purposes (Table 4.8) but at present the produce from most species and woodlands is typically used for pulp, firewood and charcoal. There may be a local demand for other, more specialised, products which can have a marked influence on the value of a crop. The figures presented in this section relate to the year 2000 when there was a recession in the timber industry.

Table 4.8 Some traditional uses of tree species grown as coppice

Species	Use
Alder	Faggots, turnery, river revetments and piles, clogs, charcoal.
Ash	Handles for tools, gate hurdles, wattle rods for building, tent pegs, turnery, furniture, fencing.
Birch	Faggots, besom heads and handles, horse jumps, turnery.
Field maple	Furniture, turning and carving, fence stakes.
Hazel	Faggots, hurdles, thatching wood, hedging stakes and ethers, crate rods, bean and pea sticks, barrel hoops.
Hornbeam	Cogs and pulleys, shoe lasts, piano keys.
Lime	Besom handles, bast, hop poles, turnery and carving.
Oak	Bark for tanning, cleft stakes, posts, spelk baskets, turnery, roof shingles, hedge stakes, hurdles.
Sweet chestnut	Hop poles, fencing, hurdles, trugs, bean and pea sticks.
Wych elm	Stakes, hurdles, bean and pea sticks, turnery.
Willow	Withes, bean sticks, thatching wood hurdles, barrel hoops, hedging stakes and ethers.

This list is not exhaustive and further information can be found in Tabor (1994), Howe (1991), Brooks (1980), Edlin (1973) and Porter (1990). Most species were also used for production of charcoal and burnt as firewood although some species were preferred (Broad, 1998).

Whatever the species or age, coppice is normally sold standing either by private treaty or tender, or more rarely by public auction. Price depends on species, quality, age and size, but just as importantly the availability of local markets and craftsmen. Road access, particularly to isolated farm woodlands, and restrictions imposed by sporting interests, also influence price.

Coppice woodlands can be conveniently classified into the 3 major types: hazel, sweet chestnut, and other coppice which are briefly discussed below.

Hazel coppice

Hazel has a wide range of uses and was a valuable component in all coppices where it was found, but it was only in the southern counties such as Wiltshire, Dorset and Hampshire, where sheep farming predominated, that hazel coppice seems to have been promoted above all other types. It is in these areas that the best hazel, and the craftsmen who use it for hurdle and spar making, are still found today.

At present, well-stocked, in-cycle hazel coppice is a valuable commodity, but if allowed to grow beyond its normal rotation it becomes a worthless liability. Unlike many other coppice species hazel will not grow into a tree but remains a large understorey shrub rarely attaining 10 m in height. Whereas for most species out-of-cycle coppice can at least be cut over at cost for production of firewood or pulp, hazel costs between £1000 and £1750 ha[-1] to restore, depending on stocking and disposal of waste. There are large areas of neglected hazel, but with grant support from local authorities such as Hampshire and West Sussex County Councils, and more recently the Forestry Commission's Woodland Improvement Grants (WIGs), much hazel is being restored and brought back into cycle.

There is an increasing demand for produce from in-cycle hazel coppice which is illustrated by the annual auctions that have recently been revived by the Wessex Coppice Group[1]. In the late 1990s and 2000 the price for 7-year-old crops of Grade 1 hazel containing at least 25 000 rods ha[-1] realised £2500 ha[-1] which, given the short rotation, represents a better return than most plantation crops. The value of the crop harvested will depend on the size and number of rods and the markets available, but a typical assortment for Grade 1 coppice 7–8 years old with 25 000 rods ha[-1] is shown in Table 4.9. This will take a coppice worker approximately 15 weeks to fell, trim out and work up into finished bundles for sale.

[1]The Wessex Coppice Group is a local authority-funded training and marketing organisation supporting the coppice industry. In 2000 it had more than 500 craftsmen on its database but not all of these work full-time in the woods.

Table 4.9 Product, unit cost and total value crop of 25 000 5 m rods of Grade 1 hazel coppice

Number	Product	Length (m)	Unit cost (pence)	Value (£)
10 000	Hurdle round rods	2–3	12	1200
5 000	Ethers[a] for hedging	3–4	24	1200
12 000	Hurdle rods for splitting	3–4	25	3000
3 000	Straight hurdle sail rods[b]	1.5–2	25	750
2 000	Hedge stakes	1.75	25	500
10 000	Spar gads[c]	0.75	10	1000
10 000	Pea sticks		12	1200
500	Bean sticks	2.50	20	100
Total				**8950**

[a]Top binders used in hedge laying.
[b]Straight rods for the uprights in hurdles.
[c]Round rods which are split into 4–8 thatching spars.

Converting the stems harvested 7 years after restoring neglected hazel coppice.

In addition to hurdles and thatching spars there is currently a big demand for hazel hedgelaying stakes and ethers (top binders), also woven garden furniture such as rose arbours and seats, trellis and flower supports. However, the use of some traditional products such as bean and pea sticks are declining as the labour cost of gathering these makes them a luxury item, rather than utilitarian garden products as in the past. One product that has recently been revived is the humble faggot: a bundle of bushy twigs usually 2 m long x 0.5 m in diameter. Thousands of these, made of mainly hazel or birch, are being used annually by the Environment Agency for river improvement works in stabilising riverbanks.

Sweet chestnut coppice

Sweet chestnut was widely planted in the Wealden coppice woodlands of Kent, Sussex and Surrey in the late 18th and 19th centuries to supply the expansion of hop farming with the tall straight poles required for growing the vine: smaller areas were established elsewhere such as Herefordshire, Worcestershire and Gloucestershire.

The wood is strong and durable, and it was an important species for post and rail fencing; since the advent of cheap wire it has been used extensively for chestnut paling although markets have declined substantially in recent years. There were many other uses, including hurdles, walking sticks and tent pegs but many of these have disappeared. It was, until recently, the most profitable of all coppice crops with prices peaking in the 1980s at £2500 ha^{-1} when 1500 people were employed in the industry. It was a very cheap crop to grow with costs being mainly restricted to ride maintenance and auction fees. However, at the end of the 1980s the markets collapsed, and prices have only recently started to return to the levels of 1970. Although there remain large areas of sweet chestnut coppice much of it is neglected and out of rotation, such woodlands often comprise multi-stemmed stored-coppice stools that will generally produce materials of only low value.

Other coppice

This category includes those woods which may be complex mixtures of species, and those which may be dominated by a single species – such as oak or alder. Many of these woods are neglected or managed as nature reserves. When managed on rotations of 15–25 years they generally produce only low value, bulk volume products such as firewood, pulpwood and charcoal. However local markets such as those provided by the few surviving turnery mills are important. Annual returns on these woodlands are usually very low but for many woodland owners these are offset by other factors such as conservation or sporting interests.

Summary

- Sites should be assessed carefully in order to decide whether coppice is the best form of management and, if so , there should be sufficient stools to achieve objectives.

- Fell during the dormant winter period using appropriate tools to make clean sloping cuts which have a generally southerly aspect.

- Cut maiden stems close to the ground and keep established stools compact by making new cuts close to the height of the previous cut. Do not cut into old wood.

- High forest can be created from coppice by use of stored-coppice, and although growth and form of this can be improved by singling, the quality of stems will probably be less than that of maidens grown in high forest.

- Restocking can be carried out by layering, natural regeneration or planting.

- Harvesting operations should minimise damage to stools and standards.

- The produce from most neglected coppice woodlands is typically used for pulp, firewood or charcoal but well-managed crops of some species can have high value although this will often depend on local markets.

Further reading and references

BEGLEY, L.D. AND COATES, A.E. (1961).
    Estimating yield of hardwood coppice for pulpwood growing. In: *Forestry Commission Report on Forest Research for the year ended March, 1960*. HMSO, London, 189–196.
BRITISH STANDARDS INSTITUTION (1984).
    British Standard Nursery Stock Part 4. Specification for forest trees. British Standards Institution, London.
BROAD, K. (1998).
    Caring for small woods. Earthscan Publications Ltd, London.
BROOKS, A. (1980).
    Woodlands: a practical conservation handbook. British Trust for Conservation Volunteers Ltd, Reading.
CROCKFORD, C.J. AND SAVILL, P.S. (1991).
    Preliminary yield tables for oak coppice. *Forestry* **64**, 29–50.

DAVIES, R. J. (1987).
Trees and weeds. Forestry Commission Handbook 2. HMSO, London.

EDLIN, H.L. (1973).
Woodland crafts in Britain. David and Charles, Newton Abbot.

EDWARDS, P.N. (1983).
Timber measurement. A field guide. Forestry Commission Booklet 49. HMSO, London.

EVANS, J. (1984).
Silviculture of broadleaved woodland. Forestry Commission Bulletin 62. HMSO, London.

EVANS, J. (1988).
Natural regeneration of broadleaves. Forestry Commission Bulletin 78. HMSO, London.

FORESTRY COMMISSION (1990).
Forest nature conservation guidelines. HMSO, London.

FORESTRY COMMISSION (1992).
Lowland landscape design guidelines. HMSO, London.

FORESTRY COMMISSION (1994).
Forest landscape design guidelines. HMSO, London.

FORESTRY COMMISSION (1994).
Forests and water guidelines. Forestry Commission, Edinburgh.

FORESTRY COMMISSION (1994).
The management of semi-natural woodlands. Forestry Commission Practice Guides 1–8. Forestry Commission, Edinburgh.

FORESTRY COMMISSION (1995).
Forest and archaeology guidelines. Forestry Commission, Edinburgh.

FORESTRY COMMISSION (1998).
Forest and soil conservation guidelines. Forestry Commission, Edinburgh.

FORESTRY COMMISSION (1998).
The UK forestry standard: the government's approach to sustainable forestry. Forestry Commission, Edinburgh.

HAMILTON, G.J. (1998).
Forest mensuration. The Stationery Office, London.

HARMER, R. (1999).
Creating new native woodlands: turning ideas into reality. Forestry Commission Information Note 15. Forestry Commission, Edinburgh.

HARMER, R. (1999).
Using natural colonisation to create or expand new woodlands. Forestry Commission Information Note 23. Forestry Commission, Edinburgh.

HARMER, R. AND KERR, G. (1995).
Natural regeneration of broadleaved trees. Research Information Note 275. Forestry Commission, Edinburgh.

HARRINGTON, C.A. (1984).
Factors influencing initial sprouting of red alder. *Canadian Journal of Forest Research* **14**, 357–361.

HERBERT, R., SAMUEL, S. AND PATTERSON, G. (1999).
Using local stock for planting native trees and shrubs. Forestry Commission Practice Note 8. Forestry Commission, Edinburgh.

HIBBERD, B.G. (1991).
Forestry practice. Forestry Commission Handbook 6. HMSO, London.
HOWE, J. (1991).
Hazel coppice, 1st edn. Hampshire County Council, Winchester.
INSLEY, H. (1988).
Farm woodland planning. Forestry Commission Bulletin 80. HMSO, London.
JEFFERS, J.N.R. (1956).
The yield of hazel coppice. In: *Utilisation of hazel coppice*. Forestry Commission Bulletin 27. HMSO, London, 12–18.
KERR, G. AND EVANS, J. (1993).
Growing broadleaves for timber. Forestry Commission Handbook 9. HMSO, London.
MACDONALD, B. (1986).
Practical woody plant propagation for nursery growers. BT Batsford Ltd, London.
MUMMERY, C. AND TABOR, R (1978).
Essex Woodlands in Trust. Essex Naturalists' Trust (quoted in Brooks, 1980).
POORE, A. (1982).
Coppice management in East Anglian woodlands and its application in urban fringe nature conservation. *Arboricultural Journal* 6, 81–94.
PORTER, V. (1990).
Small woods and hedgerows. Pelham Books, London.
POTTER, M. (1991).
Tree shelters. Forestry Commission Handbook 7. HMSO, London.
PYATT, D.G. AND SUAREZ, J.C. (1997).
An ecological site classification for forestry in Great Britain. Forestry Commission Technical Paper 20. Forestry Commission, Edinburgh.
RODWELL, J. AND PATTERSON, G. (1994).
Creating new native woodlands. Forestry Commission Bulletin 112. HMSO, London.
ROLLINSON, T.J. AND EVANS, J. (1987).
The yield of sweet chestnut coppice. Forestry Commission Bulletin 64. HMSO, London.
SAVILL, P. (1991).
The silviculture of trees used in British forestry. CAB International, Wallingford.
STANLEY, J. AND TOOGOOD, A. (1981).
The modern nurseryman. Faber and Faber, London.
TABOR, R. (1994).
Traditional woodland crafts. Batsford, London.
TUBBY, I. AND ARMSTRONG, A. (2002).
Establishment and management of short rotation coppice. Forestry Commission Practice Note 7 (revised). Forestry Commission, Edinburgh.
WILLIAMSON, D.R. (1992).
Establishing farm woodlands. Forestry Commission Handbook 8. HMSO, London.
WATKINS, C. (1990).
Woodland management and conservation. David and Charles, Newton Abbot.

WILLOUGHBY, I. AND CLAY, D. (1996).
Herbicides for farm woodlands and short rotation coppice. Forestry Commission Field Book 14. HMSO, London.

WILLOUGHBY, I. AND CLAY, D. (1999).
Herbicide update. Forestry Commission Technical Paper 28. Forestry Commission, Edinburgh.

WILLOUGHBY, I. AND DEWAR, J. (1995).
The use of herbicides in the forest. Forestry Commission Field Book 8. HMSO, London.

The shaded conditions caused by the large oak standards on this site have adversely affected growth of the hazel coppice which has developed into a very poor crop.

5. Management of Standards

Oak has always been the main species used as a standard, growing with a wide variety of species in the underwood, but the censuses carried out last century showed that standards of many other species could be found including ash, sweet chestnut, birch, beech and elm. The original role of standards was to provide large timber. During the reign of Henry VIII they were considered so important that a law was passed to control their felling, ensuring that a minimum of 12 young standards were left on each acre (i.e. 30 per hectare). At present, standards growing in coppices are also valued for their role in conservation, biodiversity, landscape and amenity.

Systematic management of standards

Although there were laws that regulated the minimum number of standards to be retained within coppice woodland, well-defined systematic procedures to control yield that were developed on the continent were probably not widely used in Britain. The fundamental principle of the method is that the number of trees in each age class should be approximately half of that in the younger class with about 50–100 standards per hectare of all age classes, most of which should be young: a possible age class structure is shown in Table 5.1. When the underwood is felled at the end of each rotation the mature trees (age class IV) are felled, new standards (age class I) are recruited and intermediate ages thinned. The number of coppice cycles for which a standard is retained depends on species, length of coppice cycle, growth rate and size of timber required: for mixed coppice on a 20-year rotation typical life-times for ash may be 3–5 coppice rotations (60–100 years) whereas those for oak may be longer: 5–6 rotations (100–120 years).

It is unlikely that standards could always be managed with such precision and in woodlands where landscape, amenity and conservation are important objectives it may be unachievable or undesirable.

Table 5.1 Number of standards of different age classes in coppice cut on a rotation of 20 years (data adapted from Crowther and Evans, 1986)

Age class	Coppice rotation	Number of stems to remain (ha⁻¹)	Approximate canopy cover (m²)	
			Average tree	Total
I	1	50	20	1000
II	2–3	30	33	1000
III	3–4	13	77	1000
IV	4–6	7	143	1000
Total		100		4000

Influence of standards on growth of the underwood

The adverse effect of standards on the growth of coppice is well known and is related to the canopy cover and shade cast. Data in Figures 5.1 and 5.2 show the influence of oak standards on some characteristics of hazel coppice. Measurements of the diameter of the tallest stem, the stool's girth, and the number of live stems present on a stool, show that for all ages of coppice, those measurements for stools growing beneath the canopy of standard trees are smaller than those in the open. The location of stools beneath the canopy of a standard also has an adverse effect on the height of the tallest stem on a stool.

Silvicultural systems of coppice with standards describe the management of standards in terms of stem numbers rather than size of individual tree's canopies and the amount of shade cast (see Table 5.1). Under traditionally managed coppice with standard woodlands most standards should be young and small, and cast little shade compared with those which are old, large and cast a lot of shade. In neglected coppice woods, particularly those comprising hazel with oak standards, the underwood is strongly suppressed by overmature standards with very large

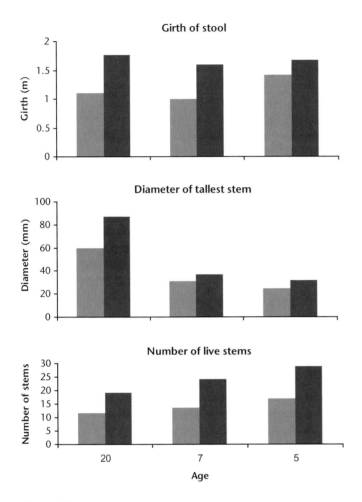

Figure 5.1

A variety of characteristics were assessed on hazel stools located either beneath or away from the canopy of standard oak trees. The shoots on the stools had 5, 7 and 20 or more years of regrowth following the last cut. The girth of the stool was measured at ground level, the total number of live shoots on each stool counted and the diameter of the longest stem on each stool measured. The light purple bars are for stools beneath the canopy; dark purple bars are for those away from the canopy. For all three characteristics, whatever the age of the coppice shoots, those stools growing beneath the canopy were smallest.

crowns, and it is rarely worth cutting coppice growing beneath the crowns as new stems will often be branched, of poor quality and regrowth will be weak. There may be few standards per hectare but they can cast considerable shade, and it is important when managing these woodlands to cut old standards and encourage smaller, younger trees, either by promoting coppice stems, planting or natural regeneration. The total amount of canopy cover remaining after felling will depend on the objectives of management: Crowther and Evans (1986; Table 5.1) suggest

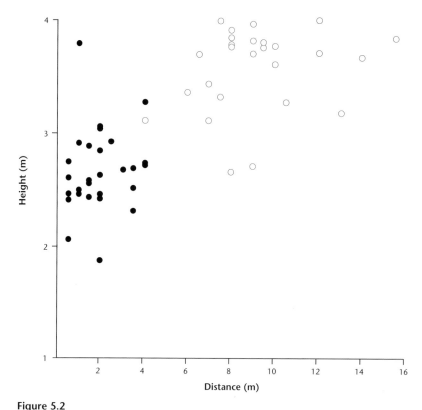

Figure 5.2

The height of the tallest hazel shoot after 5 years' regrowth was generally greater for stools located away from the canopy of overstorey oaks (● = stools beneath canopy; ○ = stools away from canopy).

40% which is somewhat higher than the 30% often recommended for conservation coppice and the 20% or less which may be appropriate for the encouragement of butterflies. The best yields and growth of coppice will occur on well-stocked sites with low canopy cover; after felling 25–30% cover is probably the maximum acceptable although small amounts of 15–20% are probably better.

Species differ in the amount of shade that they cast, varying in both size of crown produced and the density of leaf cover within the crown: trees such as beech, lime and to a lesser extent oak have very dense crowns that can cast heavy shade, whereas those of ash and birch are open and may be more suitable for use as standards. This will affect the density of standards of each species that can be maintained with a woodland.

Standards can be incompatible with growth and management of coppice and under present conditions, in which most timber is produced within high forests, they may

A recently cut coupe of hazel coppice after one season's regrowth. Too many standards have been retained and canopy cover is about 50–60% of the site.

be unnecessary if the objective of management is to produce a specialised crop such as hazel coppice on short rotations. If it is thought desirable to have overstorey standards within such productive coppice then they should be grouped on a small area, not distributed evenly throughout the site. This will simplify management of both the coppice crop and the standards. The distribution of standards on coppice sites cut for conservation, firewood or charcoal that are on irregular or long rotations will be less important, especially if the coppice species has some shade tolerance and the potential to form an overstory tree. Where landscape, amenity and the overall appearance of woodland cover are important, rather than the quality and quantity of crop produced, then an even distribution of standards is probably appropriate. Whatever their distribution, large standards should be cut at appropriate times with replacements grown as necessary.

In coppice woodlands managed for conservation the standards increase the range of habitats available, for example the retention of large, old trees substantially beyond their normal silvicultural rotation can provide deadwood, nesting holes for woodpeckers and growing sites for lichens associated with old trees. In some circumstances it may be appropriate to allow some short-lived trees such as birch, cherry and willow to become standards as these will mature and produce deadwood habitats more quickly than longer-lived species such as oak. However, too much cover from retained standards will have an adverse effect on the conservation benefits that the open-space provided by coppicing has for wildlife.

Summary

- Standards have an adverse effect on the growth of coppice and it is important when managing these woodlands to reduce the canopy cover of standards to a level that will allow satisfactory growth of the coppice underwood.

- Most standards should be young and small with few old, large trees. The number acceptable and their distribution will vary with species and management objectives. Standards are valuable in woodlands managed for conservation but overall canopy cover should not exceed 20–30% at the time of felling the underwood.

Further reading and references

BUCKLEY, G.P. (1992).
   Ecology and management of coppice woodlands. Chapman and Hall, London.
CROWTHER, R.E. AND EVANS, J. (1986).
   Coppice. Forestry Commission Leaflet 83. HMSO, London.
FORESTRY COMMISSION (1994).
   The management of semi-natural woodlands. Forestry Commission Practice Guides 1–8. Forestry Commission, Edinburgh.
FULLER, R. J. AND WARREN, M.S. (1993).
   Coppiced woodlands: their management for wildlife, 2nd edn. Joint Nature Conservation Committee, Peterborough.
MATTHEWS, J.D. (1989).
   Silvicultural systems. Oxford University Press, Oxford.
NISBET, J. (1902).
   English coppices and copse woods. *Journal of the Board of Agriculture*, 293–305 and 479–488.
PETERKEN, G.F. (1996).
   Natural woodland. Cambridge University Press, Cambridge.

RACKHAM, O. (1980).
Ancient woodland. Edward Arnold, London.
WATKINS, C. (1990).
Woodland management and conservation. David and Charles, Newton Abbot.
WARREN, M. , CLARKE, S. AND CURRIE, F. (2001).
The Coppice for Butterflies Challenge: a targeted grant scheme for threatened species. *British Wildlife* **13**, 21–28.

Unprotected stools of hazel coppice, during the second growing season after felling, with new shoots showing evidence of repeated browsing damage.

6. Protection from Browsing Mammals

The damaging effects of animals on regrowth of shoots from coppice stools has been known for many years and in the 15th and 16th centuries laws were passed to try to ensure that animals did not damage new coppice growth. The laws primarily concerned the exclusion of livestock, which at present is relatively easy in comparison to deer, rabbits and hares which are the damaging animals of major importance over much of the country. Browsing can retard regrowth and, where it is severe and prolonged, kill stools. As species show different susceptibilities to browsing the frequency and abundance of those present within the woodland may change. For example, on wet sites under moderate browsing pressure, palatable species such as ash and hazel may be suppressed to a greater extent than alder. Damage to hazel, which causes growth of crooked stems, can have a marked impact on the value of the crop. Adequate measures to protect stools from browsing after cutting are generally the most important operations needed to ensure successful re-growth from viable stools; they include controlling the populations of deer and rabbits, and physical exclusion of animals.

Before introduction of management by coppicing it is important to estimate the extent of browsing damage that is likely to occur, what species of animals are present, how many are there and what measures are needed to prevent unacceptable amounts of damage. The level of protection provided varies with the method used (Table 6.1). The amount of protection needed will vary depending on objectives,

Table 6.1 Percentage of sites 2–3 years after felling with
different types of protection and the percentage
of stools that were browsed.

Type of protection	% Sites	% Stools browsed
None	63	35
Brash piles	12	53
Dead hedge	12	12
Deer fence	8	11
Stock fence	4	4

Data from survey of 49 sites in southern England.

species and numbers of animals, and crop being coppiced: not all sites will require
the same protection, not all methods are suitable against all species of animal, and
more than one method may be required. Protection may be provided by physical
barriers, fences, guards etc., all of which should supplement the control of animal
populations.

Population control

Reducing and maintaining populations of animals at levels below those at which
unacceptable levels of damage occur, will often require a sustained effort over a long
period of time. For deer this will probably require the co-operation of neighbouring
landowners and managers.

In any woodland an acceptable deer population is one that the site can sustain
without preventing the management objectives of the site from being achieved. The
acceptable population level will vary between sites and be influenced by species of
deer and coppice stools present, the quality of the habitat and the availability of
alternative food plants. Deer culling must be carried out safely, legally and
humanely, and should concentrate on the removal of mature females. About 20–25%
of adults need to be shot each year to prevent the population from increasing.

Rabbits are best controlled by fumigating burrow systems. As the chemicals used
can be hazardous to the operator this method should only be carried out by fully
trained and equipped personnel. Although rabbits can also be trapped or shot these
methods are not suitable for eradicating large populations.

Use of harvesting residues

Protection can be gained by using branch wood remaining after harvesting. Although this can be cheap it is not reliable and may only be possible on sites receiving their first cut after a long period of neglect. On sites with in-cycle hazel coppice, where most of the crop is used, there is unlikely to be sufficient material to provide adequate protection to ensure re-growth of a high quality crop.

Cutting to waste

The cheapest and simplest option is to cut and harvest useable material, leaving branch wood spread in a deep layer across the site. This can act as a deterrent to some deer species and coppice shoots will grow through the lop and top. However, it provides ideal cover for muntjac and rabbits, which increases the risk of damage and the difficulty of any control measures that are necessary. Dense layers of waste may also have an adverse effect on the development of the ground floor.

Coppice shoots growing through a deep layer of brash.

Brash piles

Individual stools can be protected using brash that is piled on and around them. This is more labour intensive than cutting to waste but it may be possible to give protection to some stools where quantities of waste are small. The brash piles should be tall, wide and dense enough to prevent browsing of new shoots as they emerge. Although it is not possible to give a specific size, 2 m x 2 m x 1 m (l x w x h) should be sufficient. The problems with muntjac and rabbits noted above may still apply. In addition there may be some risk to coppice shoot quality, particularly for short rotation crops.

Thick pile of brash piled over a cut stool which is providing sufficient protection to allow regrowth of coppice shoots.

A small, open pile of brash giving inadequate protection to a stool that is clearly visible with all growing shoots heavily browsed. This stool was on the same site as the one on the left.

Dead hedges

These may comprise intricate fences with branch wood interwoven between upright stakes, or simple continuous piles of brash surrounding the site. They are more labour intensive than either of the other methods using waste but properly constructed they can provide good protection. Where the hedge consists of piled brash, large amounts of material is needed to create a tall, wide and dense barrier suitable to prevent access by large deer. There is almost certain to be insufficient waste to construct a suitable brash hedge after harvesting sites that are in-rotation.

A tall, wide, dense dead hedge constructed from the branch wood remaining after harvesting mixed broadleaved coppice that is adequately protected and growing vigorously.

Methods of protection using waste branch material have the advantage of no costs for materials, and the work can be done by unskilled labour. However, they may exclude animals less reliably than fencing, and they provide ideal cover for rabbits and small deer which may also penetrate the hedges. In addition, as they decompose, the duration of their protective role is unpredictable. These methods are probably most appropriate where: rabbits are not a problem, there are large amounts of branch waste, free or cheap labour is available, the species being coppiced grow quickly and some browsing damage can be tolerated.

Fences

A wide variety of types can be built, most of which require skilled labour for their construction. As there will be some cost involved with materials and labour it is important to select the fence which is the most appropriate to exclude the browsing animals present; see Further Reading for more information.

Stock fences

Simple stock fences are inadequate to exclude deer and rabbits from recently coppiced sites. Electric fences consisting of a few line wires or plastic conducting tapes are unreliable as deer will either jump over, or push between or beneath the strands; they are also ineffective against rabbits. Electrified plastic mesh netting can be effective against rabbits.

The electric fence, which was about 1.8 m tall, failed to prevent deer from causing severe damage to the hazel stools which it enclosed. Successful regrowth was only obtained by the addition of stock mesh to the bottom half of the fence, and an additional strand of tape to the top.

Temporary deer fences

These should be of sufficient height to prevent or deter deer from jumping into the fenced area. They typically comprise a reusable barrier fixed to wires strung on posts, which may be temporary or reusable: the barrier can vary in mesh size, and be metal or plastic. Chestnut paling 1.5 m tall can be used with success and may be subject to less vandalism in sites with public access, but it is unwieldy and may not exclude small animals. Temporary fences can be very successful but may not protect against rabbits and muntjac unless mesh size is suitably small and there is no gap at ground level.

Temporary plastic mesh fencing pegged down to prevent access by small deer.

Permanent deer and rabbit fences

These represent the most reliable method of excluding animals to protect stools and their construction is well described by Pepper (1992). Skilled labour is required for their erection and material costs are high. They may be best used on extensive sites where large areas can be felled, or repeated coppicing is possible within the lifetime of the fence. It will probably not be cost effective to use permanent fences on isolated, small coupes within woodlands where working is difficult and perimeters are long relative to area.

Recently erected permanent deer and rabbit fence surrounding a newly felled plot of mixed broadleaved coppice.

Choosing appropriate protection

Whatever method is used to exclude animals it should be effective for the whole time that protection is needed to allow sufficiently good regrowth to meet the objectives of management. Cutting to waste or dead hedging may be appropriate on some small, irregularly cut coupes made for conservation purposes, where the value of the crop is of low interest, the stools are sufficiently vigorous, and some damage to regrowth is acceptable. However, on most sites whether they are cut for conservation or prod-uction purposes, fencing of either a temporary or permanent nature will be necessary to maximise the chance of success. Data for regrowth of shoots from coppice stools suggests that at least 3 years' protection will be necessary for most species to grow beyond the height at which they can be damaged by fallow deer (see Table 3.5).

Summary

• Adequate measures to protect stools from browsing damage are essential to ensure successful regrowth from viable stools. Prolonged severe browsing can ruin crops, kill stools and seriously degrade woodland.

- Protection can be provided by a number of different methods but whichever is chosen it must be sufficient to meet the management objectives for the woodland.

Further reading and references

AGATE, E. (1986).
Fencing – a practical handbook. BTCV, Wallingford.
COOKE, A.S. AND LAKHANI, K.H. (1996).
Damage to coppice re-growth by muntjac deer *Muntiacus reevesii* and protection with electric fencing. *Biological Conservation* 75, 231–238.
DRAKE-BROCKMAN, G.R. (1995).
Temporary deer fencing. Technical Development Branch Technical Note 5/95. Forestry Commission, Rugeley.
GILL, R. (2000).
The impact of deer on woodland biodiversity. Forestry Commission Information Note 36. Forestry Commission, Edinburgh.
HODGE, S. AND PEPPER, H. (1999).
The prevention of mammal damage to trees in woodland. Forestry Commission Practice Note 3. Forestry Commission, Edinburgh.
KAY, S. (1993).
Factors affecting severity of deer damage within coppiced woodlands in the south of England. *Biological Conservation* 63, 217–222.
MCKILLOP, I.G. AND DENDY, J.A. (2000).
Advice on rabbit management for growers of short rotation willow coppice. Central Science Laboratory.
MAYLE, B. (1998).
Managing deer in the countryside. Forestry Commission Practice Note 6.
MAYLE, B. A., PEACE, A.J. AND GILL, R.M.A. (1999).
How many deer? A field guide to estimating deer population size. Forestry Commission Field Book 18. Forestry Commission, Edinburgh.
PEPPER, H. (1992).
Forest fencing. Forestry Commission Bulletin 102. HMSO, London.
PEPPER, H. (1998).
The prevention of rabbit damage to trees in woodland. Forestry Commission Practice Note 2. Forestry Commission, Edinburgh.
PEPPER, H. (1999).
Recommendation for fallow, roe and muntjac deer fencing: new proposals for temporary and reusable fencing. Forestry Commission Practice Note 9. Forestry Commission, Edinburgh.

PEPPER, H.W., CHADWICK, A.H. AND BUTT, R. (1992).
  Electric fencing against deer. Research Information Note 206. Forestry
  Commission, Edinburgh.
PETLEY-JONES, L. (1995).
  Deer or butterflies. *Enact* **3**, 8–10.
POORE, A. (1995).
  Dealing with deer damage. *Enact* **3**, 15–17.
PUTMAN, R.J. (1994).
  Deer damage in coppice woodlands: an analysis of factors affecting the severity of
  damage and options for management. *Quarterly Journal of Forestry* **88**, 45–54.
RATCLIFFE, P.R. AND MAYLE, B. A. (1992).
  Roe deer biology and management. Forestry Commission Bulletin 105. HMSO,
  London.
ROBINSON, J. (1995).
  Deer, Wyre and wire! *Enact* **3**, 18–19.
TABOR, R.C.C. (1993).
  Control of deer in managed coppice. *Quarterly Journal of Forestry* **87**, 308–313.
TABOR, R.C.C. (1999).
  Effectiveness of chestnut paling fencing as a protection for coppice against
  browsing by fallow, *Dama dama*, and muntjac, *Muntiacus reevesii*, deer.
  Quarterly Journal of Forestry **93**, 197–203.

Alder coppice in 3rd season of growth after felling. The stools were about 3 m in girth and had been neglected for many years. Prior to cutting there were about 3 stems on each and the remaining stumps on the stools were about 40 cm diameter.

7. Establishment of New Coppice Woodlands

Creation of new coppice woodlands by planting or direct sowing of seed has a long history and at present the establishment of large areas of short rotation coppice comprising willow or poplar for energy production is being actively promoted. New areas of traditional coppice are likely to be small but they can play an important role in the expansion and linking of ancient semi-natural woodlands, game management and amenity. Well-managed new coppice woodlands having trees with a diversity of height, diameter and age classes, that give environments with different light, moisture and temperature regimes, will provide a range of habitats with the potential to enhance biodiversity in comparison to newly planted high forest woodlands that are often even-aged with little structural variation.

Although it is relatively easy to establish the trees and shrubs which form the structural component of coppice woodlands, much of the interest of existing woodlands derives from the flora and fauna that lives within them: unless these additional species can disperse to the new coppice woodlands then they may not fulfil their potential. The rate at which many species of woodland plants invade new sites is often slow and it can take several decades for them to colonise new woodlands. If new coppice woodlands are wanted for conservation purposes then they are probably best sited next to existing semi-natural woodlands.

Simple coppice of a single species is the easiest to manage, and probably the most appropriate for those interested in the crop produced, but mixed coppice with standards has the greatest structural and age diversity, and is probably best for conservation purposes where silvicultural difficulties may be less important. However, unless there is a long-term commitment to management of new woodland as coppice, the recent history of neglect of traditional coppice suggests that it would be better to establish new high forest.

Species choice for new coppice woodlands

The species that will grow on any site will depend on its location, varying with soil type and climate. The selection of suitable species can be made from experience; observation of other woods within the locality – particularly when planting next to an existing woodland; by using information in FC Bulletin 112: *Creating new native woodlands* (Rodwell and Patterson, 1994) the National Vegetation Classification or other publications; the recently developed decision support system for Ecological Site Classification may also be helpful. However, not all species that grow on a site are suitable for inclusion in coppice woodlands either as standards or underwood. Very little is known about minor species. There is old information that suggests that some of the smaller shrubby species will not survive well in woodlands cut on a cycle of 10 years or less, but the reliability of this is unclear.

Characteristics of British tree species that can be grown as coppice stools

Alder

Alder has undemanding soil requirements but does best on moist or wet soils where pH is more than 6. It is best grown on long rotations of 25–30 years. Although stools should normally be cut close to the ground they can be cut high (50–150 cm) where flooding is a problem. On favourable soils the stools are long-lived and will re-sprout when more than 50-years-old, but on unfavourable sites that are too dry they may only survive one or two cuts. Extraction from wet sites can be difficult and is best carried out during the driest months. Regrowth from well-established stools is rapid and shoots seem less palatable to deer than those of other species.

Ash

Ash grows best on moist, fertile calcareous loams. It is suitable for underwood rotations of 10–25 years and can also be used as a standard. There is disagreement about stool longevity: some authors suggest they are short lived, surviving about 50 years or 2–3 rotations, whilst others suggest they can coppice indefinitely with some stools living for 300+ years. Ash is highly regarded as a firewood as the fresh wood contains low levels of moisture. Stored coppice rarely makes worthwhile timber as it can suffer from discoloration caused by blackheart.

Beech

Beech is generally not suitable as a coppice species but in some areas it was a traditional form of management. Coppice is only advisable on good soils which are neutral to alkaline. It responds poorly to coppicing and trees should initially be cut when they are less than 20 years old and subsequently at 10–12 year intervals. Stools can be managed on a coppice selection system. Although ages of 2–3 centuries can be attained, shoot production usually ceases after 30–40 years with stools surviving only 2–3 rotations. As it casts dense shade it should only be used as a standard after careful consideration of the management objectives.

Birch

Birch is suitable for more acid soils that may be dry and sandy. It is often regarded as a poor coppice species but it is unpredictable and results vary with soil and situation. It should be cut very close to the ground to improve chances of successful re-growth. Restoration of neglected stools often fails and it should not be grown on rotations longer than 25 years. Suitable as a standard but its prolific seed production can cause a management problem if natural regeneration is excessive. Stools are short lived and liable to die after 2–3 rotations. Crops can be harvested at 3–7 year intervals to provide small brushwood for manufacture of products such as besom broom heads and horse jumps: longer rotations of 15–20 years will provide poles for turnery.

Field maple

As field maple was not highly regarded for coppice or timber it was never planted, and its presence in an old wood may be an indication of the woodland's natural character. It grows on moist, fertile soils that are not too acidic. It is a typical underwood species that will survive well under rotations of varying length. Stools can be very long-lived achieving ages of 300 years.

Hazel

Hazel grows well on a wide variety of soil types and is generally grown on rotations of less than 10 years. Although it will survive for many years as underwood it is reported to respond poorly to re-cutting on some sites if it has been neglected for more than 50 years. When regularly coppiced the stools of this species are amongst the most durable and can live for several hundred years. There remains a good demand for a wide variety of products (see Chapter 4).

Hornbeam

Hornbeam grows on a range of soil types but does best on those that are moist and moderately fertile. This is a reliable coppice species that can be grown on rotations of 25–30 years. Although it has been found as a standard it usually casts too much shade. It has been described as indestructible with indefinite powers of regrowth, the stools being capable of surviving for centuries.

Small-leaved lime

This species was never planted as the wood was not highly regarded, being neither strong nor durable, and making poor firewood. The presence of old coppice stools is a good indicator that a wood is of ancient origin as viable seeds are produced infrequently and establishment on new sites is rare. Small-leaved lime is found on soils with a wide range of moisture, pH and nutrient characteristics. It is a very reliable coppice species that can be grown on rotations of 20–25 years, but it casts too much shade to be used as a standard. The stools can often live for several centuries, perhaps more than 1000 years.

Oak

Oak grows on a variety of soil types but is typical of moderately acid loams and clays, and coppices less reliably on sandy soils. Intolerant of shade when grown as coppice but it is a very reliable species when grown on rotations of less than 30 years, after which age its ability to regrow may decline. Oak is another species that will respond 'indefinitely' to regular coppicing, producing stools that can survive for more than 200 years. There remain small localised markets for tan bark and other traditional products such as cleft stakes, roof shingles and spelk oak baskets.

Sweet chestnut

This is a common planted species of the moderately fertile, free draining, acid soils of south-eastern England. Sweet chestnut is a very fast growing species that responds well to coppicing over rotations of 15–30 years. Stools are very durable, living for several centuries. The market for products remains but is in decline (see Chapter 4).

Sycamore

Sycamore is suitable for a wide variety of soils that are not too acidic. It grows vigorously and can be managed on rotations that do not exceed 25 years. However stools decay quickly and are short-lived, they should be cut very close to the ground to encourage new shoots to develop their own root system. It has been suggested that sycamore could be used as a standard, but it regularly produces large amounts of seed which may cause a weed problem, and crowns can be large and cast considerable shade.

Wych elm

This is the only species of elm that coppices well and is suitable for rotations of 25 years. It is generally found on moist, fertile soils that are not too acidic. Stools are very long lived. Wych elm was never popular with coppice craftsmen as the wood is difficult to cleave when small and impossible when large.

Willows

Willows require soils with good moisture availability but they respond well to coppicing, producing vigorous shoots on stools that can be long-lived. Stools can be harvested on short rotations to give small diameter stems for basket making. Selected clones grown on rotations of 2–4 years are used as biofuels.

Method of establishment

Planting is the most reliable method of achieving satisfactory establishment of trees and shrubs on a wide variety of sites. If conservation is an important objective then it may be beneficial to use plants grown from seed of local origin. Natural colonisation from nearby woodlands is possible and does have the advantage of using local genotypes, but it is too unpredictable to ensure success and cannot be recommended for the establishment new coppice. On a small scale it is possible to transplant naturally regenerated seedlings during the dormant season. Willow can be established by planting dormant hardwood cuttings.

Distribution of trees

The planting density and distribution of trees on the site will depend on a variety of factors including species, rotation length and type of woodland required. Sufficient plants should be used to allow for mortality during establishment and early coppicing treatments. As the interest in many coppices relates to the ground flora, canopy cover should develop quickly to suppress light demanding non-woodland species and provide shaded conditions under which desirable woodland plant species can establish. Initial planting densities should be a minimum of 2500 ha^{-1} (*c.* 2 x 2 m spacing) which, assuming 20–30% mortality during establishment and the introduction of the coppice regime, will leave 1750–2000 stools ha^{-1}. This is towards the upper end of the range for established coppice woods managed on short rotations of 7–10 years. Stool numbers can be reduced after establishment of the coppice wood if longer rotations are wanted. Any standards should be planted in groups to simplify their management.

Size of new woodlands

New coppice woodlands must be of sufficient area to meet their objectives whether these be primarily conservation or production. Overall size will depend on a variety of factors including:

- Length of the rotation: this will vary with species, site and product but should not exceed 25–30 years after which time viability and vigour of regrowth may decline.

- Size of the coupes: individual coupes must be of practical size and shape for efficient working, producing sufficient crop and economies of scale – for example fencing to protect from browsing after cutting. Current management guidelines suggest coupe sizes of 0.4–2.0 ha depending on woodland type, its size and location.

- Number of different age classes of coppice: this will depend on factors such as how regularly the crop is required, or for conservation management, for what the woodland is being managed.

- Whether the wood is managed as a separate unit or part of an existing woodland: new woodlands managed as part of another unit can be smaller and of a size to complement existing silviculture.

Examples

Assuming that 0.4 ha is the minimum viable size for a coppice coupe then:

A. Ash on a rotation of 20 years, where conservation requires 5 age classes, or a crop is needed every 4 years, then 0.4 x 5 = 2.0 ha of coppice is needed.

B. Hazel on a 7-year rotation, where both conservation and production need 0.4 ha to be cut every year, requires 0.4 x 7 = 2.8 ha of new coppice.

Initiation of new stools and the coppice cycle

Plants should not be cut until they have become well established and will out-grow any other vegetation that develops after the coppicing treatment. The length of time before cutting will vary with:

- species;
- size of tree originally planted;
- method of establishment;
- site type;
- vigour of the cut tree, and the new shoots and weeds that are likely to grow.

Although cutting will be possible after 1 year of growth, 3–4 years is probably a more realistic minimum, but a decision can only be made by observing the performance of plants on each site. Subsequently, cutting will be determined by the length of the rotation. For example, on good sites hazel can be cut 3 years after planting and a usable crop of poles obtained a minimum of 7–9 years later. However, it is likely to take several rotations to achieve full productivity.

Introduction of the coppice cycle to give coupes of different age can begin immediately the plants are satisfactorily established. Within new woodlands of species that respond well to cutting, such as ash, hazel and oak, the first cut of new plants can probably be deferred until they are about 20 years old. However, for species such as birch and beech that respond less well to cutting, the initial treatment of all maidens should be made when they are young and most likely to regrow.

The integration of standards within the new woodland will complicate silviculture and several approaches are possible. For ease of management and more reliable maintenance of a robust understorey the standards should be planted and managed in groups or strips, but this may be influenced by landscape criteria. Standards are cut in a cycle that is a multiple of the rotation length for the understorey, trees will be cut at about 20-year intervals with the oldest remaining for 4–5 rotations and living for 80–100 years. They should be planted in a few groups within each coupe to give a canopy cover that will not exceed 30–50% of the canopy area at the end of the rotation. For example, establish groups of 5–12 future standards by planting trees at 2 m spacing no closer than 20 m apart to give 25 groups of future standards per hectare. Thin the groups of standards as appropriate, eventually to a single tree. Regenerate within each coupe when standards have reached 80–100 years of age. This is a simple system but it will only give an even-aged overstorey of trees that are not very old when felled. Their age can be increased by extending the rotation but their total canopy cover should not exceed that for younger trees.

Introduction of uneven-aged standards is more difficult and can be achieved by natural regeneration, planting, or promoting coppice shoots. The latter is the simplest and can be achieved by ceasing to cut designated areas within some coupes at about 20 year intervals during the rotation. However, this has the disadvantage that standards will eventually be stored from stools 100 years or more old. Alternatively planted maidens in new woodlands can remain uncut until they reach specified ages at which they would be felled prematurely to re-establish younger standards either by natural regeneration, planting or by coppice regrowth from the maiden stumps (which is less certain the older the trees are before felling).

Whichever method is used the areas designated for standards must be properly thinned throughout growth to ensure satisfactory development of a robust tree. The introduction of an overstorey of standards is a procedure that will require a very long-term approach to woodland management, but it will produce woodlands that have structural and age characteristics of greater variety than those of simple coppice.

Summary

- The woody components of new coppice woodlands can be easy to establish but in order to maximise the likelihood of any conservation benefits the new woodlands should be placed beside an existing woodland.

- A wide variety of woody species can be planted but those chosen must be suitable for the site.

- The number of trees planted and the size of the woodland must be sufficient to achieve the management objectives for the site.

- Simple coppice will be the easiest to manage; if standards are wanted then they will be simpler to manage if they are grown in groups or strips.

- The first coppice cut should only be made when trees are properly established.

Further reading and references

FORESTRY COMMISSION (1994).
  The management of semi-natural woodlands. Forestry Practice Guides 1–8. Forestry Commission, Edinburgh.
FORESTRY COMMISSION (1998).
  The UK forestry standard: the government's approach to sustainable forestry. Forestry Commission, Edinburgh.
ARMSTRONG, A. (1999).
  Establishment of short rotation coppice. Forestry Commission Practice Note 7. Forestry Commission, Edinburgh.
DAVIES, R. J. (1987).
  Trees and weeds. Forestry Commission Handbook 2. HMSO, London.
FERRIS-KAAN, R., ed. (1995).
  The ecology of woodland creation. John Wiley and Sons, Chichester.
HARMER, R. (1999).
  Creating new native woodlands: turning ideas into reality. Forestry Commission Information Note 15. Forestry Commission, Edinburgh.
HERBERT, R., SAMUEL, S. AND PATTERSON, G. (1999).
  Using local stock for planting native trees and shrubs. Forestry Commission Practice Note 8. Forestry Commission, Edinburgh.
KERR, G. (1998).
  A review of black heart of ash (*Fraxinus excelsior* L.). *Forestry* **71**, 49–56.
PETERKEN, G.F. (1993).
  Woodland conservation and management, 2nd edn. Chapman and Hall, London.
PETERKEN, G.F. AND GAME, M. (1984).
  Historical factors affecting the number and distribution of vascular plant species in the woodlands of central Lincolnshire. *Journal of Ecology* **72**, 155–182.
POORE, A. (1982).
  Coppice management in East Anglian woodlands and its application in urban fringe nature conservation. *Arboricultural Journal* **6**, 81–94.

POTTER, M. (1991).
Tree shelters. Forestry Commission Handbook 7. HMSO, London.

PYATT, G., RAY, D. AND FLETCHER, J. (2001).
An ecological site classification for forestry in Great Britain. Forestry Commission Bulletin 124. Forestry Commission, Edinburgh.

RODWELL, J.S (1991).
British plant communities, vol. 1: *Woodlands and scrub*. Cambridge University Press, Cambridge.

RODWELL, J. AND PATTERSON, G. (1994).
Creating new native woodlands. Forestry Commission Bulletin 112. HMSO, London.

RACKHAM, O. (1990).
Trees and woodlands in the British landscape. J. M. Dent and Sons Ltd, London.

WILLIAMSON, D.R. (1992).
Establishing farm woodlands. Forestry Commission Handbook 8. HMSO, London.

WILLOUGHBY, I. AND CLAY, D. (1996).
Herbicides for farm woodlands and short rotation coppice. Forestry Commission Field Book 14. HMSO, London.

WILLOUGHBY, I. AND DEWAR, J. (1995).
The use of herbicides in the forest. Forestry Commission Field Book 8. HMSO, London.